To Steve

First published 2013
by Focal Press
70 Blanchard Road, Suite 402, Burlington, MA 01803

Simultaneously published in the UK
by Focal Press
2 Park Square, Milton Park, Abingdon, Oxon OX14 4RN

Focal Press is an imprint of the Taylor & Francis Group, an informa business

Notices
Knowledge and best practice in this field are constantly changing. As new research
and experience broaden our understanding, changes in research methods, professional
practices, or medical treatment may become necessary.

Practitioners and researchers must always rely on their own experience and knowledge
in evaluating and using any information, methods, compounds, or experiments described
herein. In using such information or methods they should be mindful of their own
safety and the safety of others, including parties for whom they have a professional
responsibility.

Product or corporate names may be trademarks or registered trademarks, and are used
only for identification and explanation without intent to infringe.

Library of Congress Cataloging in Publication Data
CIP data has been applied for.

ISBN: 978-0-240-82502-1 (pbk)
ISBN: 978-0-240-82504-5 (ebk)

Typeset in Univers by Alex Lazarou
Front cover art © Patricio Villarroel. Back cover art © Cédric Philippe.

Mobile Digital Art

Using the iPad and iPhone as Creative Tools

by

David Scott Leibowitz

Focal Press
Taylor & Francis Group

NEW YORK AND LONDON

CONTENTS

SECTION 1
THE PAINTERS

SECTION 1
THE PAINTERS

SECTION 2
PHOTOGRAPHY, COLLAGE AND PHOTOMONTAGE

SECTION 3
ABSTRACT, BACKGROUND, AND CONCEPTUAL APPS

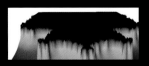

About the Author

David Scott Leibowitz brings over forty years of fascination with photography, video art, and computers to his current position as a pioneer in the developing medium of digital fine art. Mr. Leibowitz is part of a new generation of artists who are redefining the boundaries of both fine arts and popular culture. Having come of age during the information revolution, his work merges an appreciation for film, video, and photography, the plastic arts, with an affinity for the latest computer technology. Mr. Leibowitz has pursued his personal interest in creating a new visual language through the use of photography, videography, 3D renderings, and collage assembled on the Macintosh platform. At the turn of the century, he designed the searchable website Leibo.net as a living, ever changing portal into his world. It extensively documents this artist's evolution of imagery into the digital age, and is updated constantly with new work. In 2008, he began making art on a new computing platform, Apple's iPhone, and then, with its introduction, the iPad. Using dozens of apps, he is now creating art as new as the latest photo/art apps release. In 2009, he co-developed his iPhone app, "iCreated", with developer Andrew Stone, dedicated to promoting iPhone and iPad art via a gallery of international artists, and creating a visual link between mobile art and applications. Mr. Leibowitz is also one of the founding directors and board members of iAMDA, the International Association of Mobile Digital Artists, an organization formed in 2010 and dedicated to promotion and education related to mobile digital art. With a multitude of images, the latest tools and techniques, and a refined artistic sensibility, Mr. Leibowitz, camera still in hand, continues his pursuit of new methods to match new visions.

Acknowledgements

Thanks to my family whose sacrifice, dedication, and faith made the writing of this book possible. A special thanks to my son Jake for telling me about Google Translate in the very beginning of this process, which made writing this book a thousand times easier.

I'd like to thank the great minds at Apple, starting with Steve and the Woz. Between the iPhone and the iPad, Apple has provided the technology that facilitated this new art movement and binds it together. I consider myself fortunate to have lived in the Steve Jobs era and was always proud to be a an Apple fanboy. This man's vision and quest for perfection has had profound consequences on the history of computing and, ultimately, the history of mankind.

A special thanks to Andrew Stone, my co-developer in the app "iCreated". His hard work and expertise made my vision of an iPhone art app a reality. Like the miracle of creation (sorta), he built the app in six days from my initial email request to submission of the finished app to Apple. The app propelled me into this world of iPhone art, meeting artists, seeing new work every day, curating the gallery, and watching it gain recognition as a visual resource for iPhone/iPad art. The concept for this book was the same as the "iCreated" app, to create a visual correlation between art and apps. In addition to teaching technique and expert methodology, this book presents some early masterpieces and a bit of mobile digital art history, and for me it all started with Andrew C. Stone.

Last but definitely not least, I'd like to thank all the artists involved, who shared their art, their techniques, their time, and a little bit of their souls to make this book compelling

Foreword

The intent of this book is to clearly communicate how to create art on mobile devices, with multiple techniques taught by multiple experts. The reader will experience the art-making process through the eyes of seventy different artists so you too can apply these various techniques, and become inspired to make your own mobile art.

This entire book will require that you spend a few minutes getting familiar with the various apps, to know the basics of each app in each tutorial. This information is contained within each app, and since all are simple to learn, we will use the space in the book to instead teach each artist's techniques and how he/she applies these new tools to create original art. While app developers can build the tools, it is the combination of said tools and the talent these artists each bring to the table that makes the art vital and relevant. It is sometimes difficult to express in words the creative process of painting, step by step, or the thought process involved. So each artist also reveals some motivation or inspiration that will help you see their art in context to the world of art you already know and understand. Combining information about each artist, their influences, and their background will help fill in the blanks.

INTRODUCTION

I'd like to quote from the book *Paris in Our Time* (Albert Skira, Paris: Editions d'Art, 1957).

Nothing is more striking in the history of art—and indeed the history of culture in general—than the sudden breaks of continuity which take place when after a slow, sedate advance "from precedent to precedent" a more adventurous generation comes to the fore, eager for new worlds to conquer. In the case of art these bloodless revolutions are often the work of a quite small group of rebels or even a single man in whom the smoldering unrest of several generations bursts into flames.

The author was describing the transition from Realism to Impressionism around 140 years ago, when the artists of the day were freed from the constraints of their studios by the new technology of its day, paint in tubes! They went outside to paint what they saw in the real world. Their joy of discovering freedom of expression unleashed the powerful, most universally loved period of art, Impressionism. One needs only to spend some time in the Musée d'Orsay in Paris, or the Impressionist wing of the local museum, to feel the exuberance that this freedom of movement released in this prolific group of artists.

Yet this quote could describe the movement of making mobile digital art that has arrived all around the world simultaneously. The Impressionists were friends who shared their works with each other, exhibited together, shared the same philosophy, and were wholly rejected by the Salon in Paris, the art establishment of its day. It took them twenty years to gain recognition from the art establishment. iPhone artists, separated by distant locations and different languages, have found a home together on the photo-sharing network Flickr, where they share their work in groups dedicated to iPhone

and iPad paintings, photos, and collage. Over the years they have established amazing friendships and collaborations. Despite their worldwide separation, since 2010 they have exhibited together, in shows dedicated specifically to mobile art, in New York, Las Vegas, San Francisco, Chicago, Washington DC, Connecticut, Wisconsin, Maine, Toronto, Hamburg, Milan, Herzegovina, and the UK. It seems that in this day and age of instant communication, it will take mobile art considerably less time to become an accepted art medium.

But the art establishment is another story. Like any institution, the art world profits from the sale of works of established artists, whose work has a market, and a high market value. Where does the work of new artists and their new forms of art fit into this equation? With rare exceptions, it doesn't. New visions take some time to gain acceptance, and art history has taught us that it's not unusual for an artist to spend a lifetime creating art in obscurity, only to get recognition after his or her death. Today, obscurity doesn't exist for anyone with computer access or a smartphone. You have the freedom to publish your work in an ever growing number of blogs, photo-sharing networks, social networks, or your own web portal. Now, the cream rises to the top in an extremely democratic fashion.

Mobile Art—It's Not All About the Apps

The art world changed with the opening of the iTunes App Store. There have been 800,000 apps and over 40 billion downloads since the opening in July 2008. Most iPhone and iPad users acquire apps to help them find their way around, make them laugh, or amuse their friends in some way; some find apps to be useful tools they use frequently in their daily lives. Then there are the artists like me, who have hundreds of art or photography apps that they use depending on the image, the mood, and the vision. The apps "Brushes" and "SketchBook Pro" have a huge presence in this book as most of these artists came to mobile art and these popular apps from traditional painting. In 2008, the translation to this new canvas was painless and mostly playful. Since then, this art form has produced many masters and works that will no doubt one day be considered early 21st century masterpieces, as you will see in the following pages.

The App Store still provides the kid-in-the-candy-store experience for all artists and aspiring artists as new tools with new functionality appear daily, to the delight of end-users. Obviously, tools are important, but they don't do anything by themselves in the same way as a computer, a pencil, or a paintbrush doesn't. A computer is just a box and a pencil is graphite in a wooden case; like the iPhone or the iPad, they're moot without human interaction. It is the artists who extend their thinking, apply their skills and sensibilities, adapt to these new kinds of tools, and make them sing. Gauguin said, "The Painter is not the slave either of the past or the present, either of nature or his neighbor: he is always himself." In this case, each artist brings that "self" to these devices and, with the help of thousands of specialized apps, creates mobile art.

Mobile Digital Art/Art History

New art movements usually are torn from others, Realism giving way to Impressionism over the course of twenty years, Surrealism and Pop art spinning off from Dadaism five years and then fifty years later. Marcel Duchamp's readymades and Kurt Schwitters' elegant collages gave way to the Surrealists, who returned to reclaim the importance of technical proficiency. But it didn't matter, since the changes in thinking had already occurred. Now there were no rules. The Dadaists and Surrealists gave way to the Abstract Expressionists, Pop artists, and Conceptual artists, and again, there were no rules. If freedom for the artist was fundamental to these art movements, the mobile art movement in the 21st century takes artistic freedom to a whole new level. Through the sheer power of the web, which is the glue that holds it together and the fuel that drives it forward, this movement has levels of interactivity and communication that artists of the past could not have even imagined.

Some art movements are born from wars, like Dadaism, which reflected the human condition after World War I,

Abstract Expressionism, which followed World War II, and the Pop/Psychedelic art movements during the Vietnam war. Mobile art was born of technology, but in a post-9/11 world with wars in Iraq and Afghanistan. Although it's technology that's the binding force here, the movement takes place in a time when the prevailing mindset is that anything's possible, anything goes.

In the past, one could produce a chart that linked one art movement to the next, but art made on the iPhone and iPad is influenced by the diversity in the world and in the world of artists who are all sharing the same studio space. The iPhone art movement has Realists, Impressionists, Dadaists, Cubists, Surrealists, Abstract Expressionists, Pop artists, Conceptual artists, technical artists, musical artists, video artists, process artists, and is inclusive of all styles of art generated by artists worldwide. The common thread is that each artist picked up the iPhone or an iPad and made art using whatever skill set he/she brought to the iDevice.

The mobile artists' impact illustrates an important aspect of modern art, the unexpected unity created when two dissimilar concepts are combined to create a new relationship, in this case ubiquitous cellphone and fine art. For the viewer, this departure from the norm is as liberating as Duchamp's drawing a mustache on the *Mona Lisa*, maybe easier because he/she already has the technology in his/her pocket.

Sometimes the construction of a new art movement requires the destruction of another one, but here there is no destruction, just a new toolbox, with app developers vying for the masses to create with their latest and greatest tools. New technology has a long history of creating new art. In 1841, the American artist John Rand patented the first collapsible metal tube, made of tin, for artists' oil paint. Before that, artists had to be their own chemists, grinding colors and mixing them with oil and paint-thinner. To work outdoors, they had to transport their paint mixtures in leaky pig bladders, which allowed the paint to dry out quickly. Paint in tubes was the new technology of the day that drove the Impressionist artists outdoors and facilitated the creation of the most beloved movement in art history. Renoir was quoted years later, "Without paint in tubes, there would be no Impressionism." In mobile art, the leap in technology wasn't pig bladders to metal tubes, but the introduction of the iPhone and App Store.

The introduction of photography was another monumental technological shift in art history, not just as an emerging art form unto itself but to facilitate various applications within the art world. Painters used photographs as a source of accurate perspective, some even projecting the images onto canvas as reference. Then there were those who saw different possibilities for this new medium, using photography as a way to combine incongruous elements to achieve unexpected emotional content.

The Berlin Dadaists coined the term *photomontage* just after World War I. They wanted a word to describe their new technique of introducing photographs into their work and took the position that photos, text, drawing, and found scraps could all be considered a photomontage. John Heartfield, an icon in the history of photomontage, said, "A photograph can, by the addition of an unimportant spot of color, become a photomontage, a work of art of a special kind."

This kind of out-of-the-box thinking is pervasive in mobile art, where elements of photography are easily combined with text, painted elements, and anything you can find on the web. A Dadaist finds a scrap of paper on the street and uses it in his/her collage. One hundred years later, the mobile artist searches Google, pulls the relevant image off the cloud and uses it in his/her collage. It makes me wonder what the artist will be doing a hundred years from now …

What Defines Mobile Digital Art?

Usually when you try to trace the history of any art movement, it's impossible to pinpoint the exact moment it began. In the case of mobile digital art, the second the iTunes App Store opened, the mobile digital art movement was on. In July of 2008, the App Store opened with a few thousand apps, some dedicated to painting and some to photo manipulation. Artists began gravitating to this new computer platform, making art from day one. As the App Store grew, the number of apps to make art and photography multiplied exponentially. The media started to recognize the work that began popping up in different visual forums, but it was Jorge Colombo's *New Yorker* cover and David Hockney's iPhone sketches that brought worldwide attention to this new medium. Talented artists began making art exclusively on the iPhone. Although one could describe the work as an extension of digital art, since many iPhone artists began there, many more traditional artists who had never touched a computer began making art on their iPhones in droves. The introduction of the iPad further established this mobile platform as a tool for

content creation because its size makes it more acceptable to a greater range of artists.

Mobile digital art includes any works made by any artist on these devices. This includes music, video, and animation, but of course it would be hard to feature any of these mediums here in this book for obvious reasons. It is important to recognize that these alternative forms of artistic human expression are also represented, with a vast array of developers, artists, and apps to make it happen.

An art movement from the past would be defined as when a group of artists, together, create a similar style of art. Here we have a movement that is stylistically diverse yet banded together by the use of common technology. For this reason, this book has been divided into three sections that represent different stylistic approaches to these devices.

Section 1: The Painters

The painters represent the largest group of artists worldwide to pick up the iPhone and iPad for artistic reasons. Their diversity would be hard to represent, even though this book attempts it by presenting over forty traditional painters. At this point in time, it leaves out many, many talented mobile artists, easily enough to fill another book.

Section 2: Photographers, Collage, and Photomontage

Photographers were selected for their distinctive iPhone-centric approach to this new art form. Collage and photomontage artists use mobile devices to create complex compositions. This section also includes some "iPhone mash-up artists" who use multiple apps to create their mobile art.

Section 3: Abstract, Background, and Conceptual Art Apps

Art apps like kaleidoscopic apps, fractal art generators, and abstract art generators are apps many mobile artists use in the creative process. These apps are used by many artists to create stand-alone art, but are also used as part of a multi-app approach to making art. For conceptual artists, this is a new arena where the app is the art.

MOBILE ART OBSERVATIONS

Mike Nourse

ARTIST, EDUCATOR
Illinois, USA

Mike Nourse is an intermedia artist and Director of Education at the Hyde Park Art Center in Chicago.

When I was first asked to write about iPhone art in 2009, whatever iPhone art meant to the larger art world was up for debate. Now, in 2013, the song remains the same, although with thousands more apps, the growth of mobile art in general, and the explosion of online sharing, it would be hard to doubt the impact of this tool and its powerful effect on the world as we know it. Some continue to see the iPhone as a powerful art-making tool while others still see nothing more than a phone with bells. While the debate goes on, fine artists everywhere are making, sharing, and selling iPhone, mobile, and iPad art in increasing numbers. You can find iPhone art on the cover of print publications and inside online magazine articles, in galleries and in private collections, and the quality of mobile art has increased to the stage where point-and-shoot cameras are fading into the background. After a few years of international use, there's a strong case to be made that the iPhone is at worst a flexible, powerful, and convenient new tool for contemporary artists.

When I curated the first international exhibition of iPhone art in 2009, there were more doubters than believers. The artists represented the minority but, in my opinion, a very powerful one. It was relatively easy to find strong work from around the world and, more importantly, strong momentum which implied that this movement was only going to grow, which it has. Today we see a more powerful iPhone leading to incredible works of all kinds, the iPad has emerged as an outgrowth with record sales and dominance in the market, and rival phone devices have all evolved designs to feature touch-screen interfaces, access to applications, and many other iPhone characteristics. In short, the world has shown that the iPhone had it right, and today there are countless more believers than skeptics.

The iPhone, iPad, and mobile art movement will continue to impact our lives. After teaching digital media for years and an iPhone Art course in 2009, I have seen many tools and trends come and go, and the iPhone certainly falls into the category of "legitimate", if anything for the foreseeable future. Below you will find some of my thoughts on how the iPhone fits into the newer art landscape of the 21st century.

Historical Relevance

Photography is a strong example of a tool that took time to be accepted inside the world of art. What were early photographs but cheating the representational painting process? I had read about this history in college, and saw similar developments first-hand in a couple of areas. For example, music software (is digital editing a viable tool for music? many people didn't think so), then image editing software such as "Photoshop" (are digital images worthy? many people initially had doubts). I have learned that asking the question "Is this a viable art tool?" often declares the answer by itself. Yes, it is. If it were not an option for artists, we would simply not be asking the question to begin with. The iPhone and iPad's development mirrors many tools of the past, which makes me think that these devices are in fact legitimate ones for 21st century artists.

Sharing Art

Let's face it, if the art never reaches an audience, then what is the point? Mobile devices allow the user to experience sharing art in new ways (even in 2013), which provide options for artists to reach their audiences: direct communication between individuals, posting to social networking, sharing through new apps such as "Instagram", uploading to specific sites such as YouTube, Flickr, and Vimeo.

These things are all possible with mobile devices in 2013 and allow a conversation to happen, which is what defines art at its very core. In addition, artists today are responsible for all aspects of communications when it comes to their practice. Sending images or work via the internet or phone network is half of the game. The other half is following up, connecting with people, and it just so happens this tool allows you to communicate in countless ways, meaning more ways for artists to meaningfully connect with their audience.

Inspiration Leads to Creation

A tool that can capture inspirational moments can be extremely valuable. Desktop publishing allowed users to create close to home, and laptops took this a step further with portability. The iPad has built on the iPhone's success, but an iPhone (like most newer mobile devices) allows users to take a digital studio wherever they want, one that works with phone networks meaning easy access to communication. Unlike most computers or even iPads, people often *have* to take their creative device with them (because it is also their phone). This last distinction separates the iPhone and mobile devices from other digital tools.

Artists Love Saving Money

With so many apps, the artist can spend time customizing the tool for his/her needs without spending hundreds or thousands of dollars on full-blown software packages. I've personally spent about $25 total on apps since acquiring my iPhone in 2009: that's a fraction of what most creatives spend on desktop software. Even as a part-time iPhone artist I've made more than twenty-five times that selling some of my iPhone art.

Art is Enjoyment

At the end of the day, artists in general seek to enjoy their own process, and in addition to being powerful the iPhone is playful and fun to use. If you've ever enjoyed playing a video game, navigating your satellite television guide, or engaging with interactive museum exhibits, chances are you are 21st century friendly and would also enjoy an iPhone/iPad/mobile device interface. It is fun, easy to use, and can take art projects as far as you can imagine, sometimes farther.

Documentation is as Important as the Art

With a built-in camera for high-quality stills or HD video and apps for editing content, iPhones and iPads can create, edit, *and* document! Apps such as "Photoshop" allow the iUser to master still images with professional tools, as does "iMovie" with video. And using the iPad has only enhanced the experience, allowing for more space to see more details. The iPhone and the iPad present an all-in-one package that make them prolific tools, fitting perfectly inside the 21st century "do-it-yourself" culture.

The Future is Now

If anything, the proliferation of touch-pad phones over the last few years points to more options for portable art-making devices, something that keeps communications components at the forefront while adding to creative tool sets. With the Droid, Google Phone, and Fender collector phones, we see more and more companies diving into a valuable market. The iPad is also a game-changer, pushing past communications devices into its own category (although we can now connect iPads through phone networks). Armed with the same operating systems and the same sea of apps as the iPhone, it creates a new space between phone and computer to facilitate art.

In the long run, the iPhone might not maintain its place as a market leader in this area (who knows?). However, it has clearly established itself as a pioneering tool and currently sits at the head of the pack. With many years under its belt and other phone companies copying as much as possible, it is clear that this device has changed the art landscape. With so much creative potential, it's no wonder that artists in 2013 often go days without making a phone call. This tool is too powerful!

MOBILE ART FUNDAMENTALS

Craig Newsom

ARTIST, PROFESSOR
Ilinois, USA

Around us small bookstores shutter their windows, libraries desperately install coffee shops and newspapers crumble. In the meantime, each one of us, with what is commonly known as a smartphone, holds the sum total of all human knowledge and experience in the palms of our hands. We carry these tiny windows with us everywhere, hold them to our heads and stare at them, either in crowds or alone. There is an unwritten covenant that comes with these devices, an implied agreement. The covenant is one of connection. It is expected that with these devices we will never be alone and will always be able to broadcast our message to the entire world.

This book represents another aspect of the phones, pods, and pads we use to entertain ourselves with or to simply make calls with. It represents a way we can use our devices to actually make things. In this manner, we become the entertainers instead of the entertained. We can actually use our devices to connect and interact with our immediate environment. We can use our devices to locate and collaborate with like-minded individuals in different hemispheres. Hidden in many of our mobile apparatuses are music studios, video studios, and art studios. The keys to unlocking these studios are very inexpensive and sometimes free apps that can be downloaded from the devices themselves.

When I first got my iPod Touch I didn't really know what to do with it. I spent a great deal of time just looking at it. It seemed to look the best in early morning light held parallel with the ground against a bright blue sky. It was beautiful. I dutifully placed songs on it, as this was the one act I was certain I should perform. The box it came in was beautiful too. I couldn't get rid of it.

It never occurred to me that I could make anything with it. Then a funny thing happened. It's the same epiphany that happened to many of the mobile digital artists in this book. I saw the June 1, 2009, cover of *The New Yorker*. That cover had been created entirely on an iPhone with the "Brushes" app. After dowloading "Brushes", "SketchBook Mobile", and some other apps, I got rid of all the music on the iPod Touch. It would become my mobile studio. An iPhone and an iPad later, apps and devices and Wi-Fi and Bluetooth and swiping and iOS are all part of my art vernacular.

With each medium I work with, my concern always gravitates toward specificity. What can paint do that clay cannot? What can a pencil do that a paintbrush cannot? What can you do on an iPhone that you can't do on paper? While a great deal of mobile digital art leans toward emulation of more traditional methods, there are a number of aspects to working with an iThing that are unique to it. It could be argued that all of these things can be accomplished through traditional methods or on a desktop computer. But those things do not fit in your pocket. These are just a few points I've found that are helpful to my own pursuits:

Collaboration

From prehistoric people working together in caves to the Surrealists sitting in their smoke-filled parlors making exquisite corpses together, artists have been collaborating

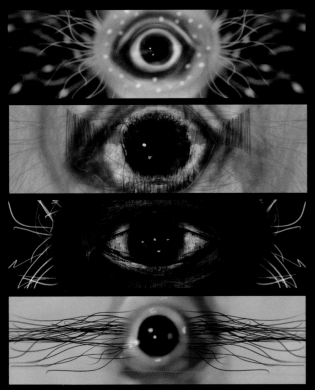

Kara Jansson Kovacev and I call our collaborative art "Coalfather Industries" (coalfather.com).

for ages. It's different on an iPhone, though, because you can collaborate immediately with another artist on the other side of the globe. Not every app allows for this. A newly introduced app called "Sketchshare" allows artists to work at exactly the same time in exactly the same spot on a piece. This is an advantage over traditional media, where two artists could not physically be drawing exactly the same line at exactly the same time.

Symmetry

Some apps, like "SketchBook Pro", allow you to create perfectly symmetrical designs. Again, there is nothing new about symmetry in the art world. But what "SketchBook Pro" allows you to do is create a line and/or form and its mirror image at exactly the same time. The ease with which this can be accomplished is remarkable. Combined with sets of different layers, this means that in a manner of minutes incredibly complex and engaging designs can be created.

Three examples of symmetry using the app "SketchBook Pro".

Fluidity

There is a fluid sense of motion and response that is absolutely unique to the movement of a finger over glass. When you are working with a well-made app, there is nothing like it. Of course, this brings up all manner of arguments that compare the familiar sounds of a pencil dragging over paper fibers to the warm sounds of dust and scratches on a vinyl record. But I don't think we need to view mobile digital methods as replacements for traditional methods. They are different. They are new tools to be used in our daily practice as artists.

Spontaneity

Ask any artist. Very often the best things happen entirely by accident. How, then, to produce accidents consistently?

"Harmony" is an online procedural drawing tool developed by Ricardo Cabello aka Mr. Doob. The great thing about "Harmony" is that it works in Safari on both the iPhone and the iPad. Its resolution depends on the size of the screen being used, though—so anything produced on the iPhone will remain quite small. The best thing about "Harmony" (and other procedural drawing tool apps) is that it is at once controllable and completely uncontrollable. As you draw, other elements or lines will spontaneously grow, form the line you are creating, and connect to lines nearby. There is no undo in "Harmony", which adds to the immediacy and sometimes frenetic nature that is inherent in it.

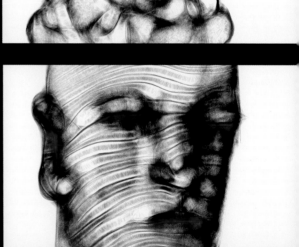

There are different ways to approach making art on an iPhone or iPad. Many have come to it with no prior experience whatsoever. A good number were practicing and exhibiting artists to begin with. It's easy to grab an iPhone and just start making something with an app like "Brushes" or "SketchBook", even if you've never picked up a paintbrush in your life. Alternatively, if you have an academic past or training in art, there are complexities and subtleties embedded in nearly every app that allow for extended exploration. Personally, as someone who was trained in both sculpture and painting, at first it was hard for me to take seriously the pieces I was making on the iPod Touch. That hesitation soon gave way when I realized the built-in proliferation in mobile digital methods and began to connect with the wider network of other artists working with the same tools and same ideas.

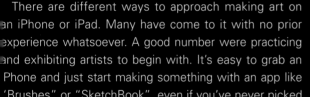

The unwritten covenant of connection, then, is upheld but in a very different way than one might expect. It turns out that communicating through images is much more effective

IN THE BEGINNING WAS A DRAWING ...
(THOUGHTS ON DRAWING AND BINARY CODE)

David Stern

New York, USA

Drawing, as much as it seems to be an action executed by hand/eye coordination and the hand's trained ability to make delicate movements with a pen or brush, is, as Michelangelo Buonarroti pointed out some 450 years ago, really an activity which takes place in the brain. Nothing shows this more clearly than if one switches materials, or uses no materials at all, as in the case of electronic drawings, where all the drawing is done through binary coding, arranging pixels on a screen.

In a way this is the only technique to make a truly flat work of art, since these pixels are only arranged side by side and each drawing mark indicates a decision between 0 and 1: there are no gray areas, as in the ordinary human experience, and there are no maybes or ambiguities. It's yes or no, black or white. Neal Stephenson, in his essay "In the Beginning was the Command Line", equates the binary code to a God-like quality. The writer of the code needs to know exactly what he wants the computer to do, and only then does the magic work, and we non-hackers see, through our GUI glasses, a spreadsheet or drawing developing.

I am not writing code, I am just using a graphic user interface (GUI) in its most advanced form as an iPhone app, with my right-hand middle finger drawing things, figures, portraits, and scenes, some done directly from observation, others from imagination. It is surprising that this mediated technology allows for a spontaneous and propriety drawing behavior. The drawings I have made with it so far all show the same "hand-writing" as my on paper sketches and drawings; considering that I do not normally draw with a

bare finger but rather with graphite sticks and pencils, it gives evidence to Michelangelo's statement: "A man paints with his brain and not with his hands."

But drawing is also visualizing concepts and ideas. Even the simple act of drawing an object or figure from life is

such a visualization: by choosing the object, the angle, the trajectory of the line, etc., a concept or idea of the object or figure is formulated. It is important to understand that by drawing a figure we are not making it, or creating an illusion of it, but visualizing an idea of that figure in a different world, so to speak. In the case of electronic drawings one could call it a flatland world. There seems to be an inherent connection between drawing and binary code in the sense that both are used as abstracting measures, creating an interface which allows for the expression of ideas and the transmission of information. Drawing is a lot like binary code in the sense that it also is a "yes and no" decision-making process. Either there is a line or there is none; there are no gray areas, not even in shading a figure drawing; it is always about whether to let the empty space (non-mark or NO or 0) speak or choosing the line (mark or YES or 1). So in that way drawing, and much more so electronic drawing, is a quite pure form of creation, mimicking the ultimate creation of "something out of nothing".

It is an interesting question where and whether an electronic drawing really exists in its electronic form as binary code. It becomes clear, when it is printed or displayed on a screen, that the information has been somewhere (I guess on a memory chip occupying some virtual or real space?) but is that really a physical or rather a metaphysical existence? Or is it a combination of real and virtual in the way that the drawing is somewhere in its potentiality, but realizes only if given the command to display in some form of material media? In a way that seems to be a satisfying concept, mirroring the human condition it's in—between the status of potential and realization and eventually transformation, where one could say that all three stages signify some kind of existence on some level.

And then there is the magic of the interfacing apps I am using to draw on my iPhone, which allow me not only to take steps back and forth, but also to record these steps as a screen video, which is like an old painter's dream coming true: to be able to see whether one actually makes progress by continuing to work on a piece.

Some thirty years ago I had long instructional conversations with E. Bert Hartwig, then already a senior painter, who in turn got his instructions at the Bauhaus from Paul Klee. He reported that some Bauhaus masters made a point of using photography to record the daily changes they made on a painting or drawing; how great it would be to see the actual process of creation unadulterated by one's own consciousness of having a camera behind, recording every step one makes. In a surprising way, touch-screen technology has made all of this possible. Contrary to the technology phobia of the 1960s and 1970s, which expressed enormous anxiety about the potential death of all creativity and human expression through technology, and mostly information technology, it has rather provided an unprecedented freedom from material boundaries—a freedom we have only begun to comprehend and put into use in the creative and artistic process.

Section 1

The Painters

The Painters are at the core of this movement; this worldwide group of traditional artists who all simultaneously discovered a new passion for painting on their iPhones. This group knows no geographical boundaries; they are tied together by the web. The established artists were joined by others learning these new tools, so one's stature in the art world mattered less here. All that matters is the art.

The talented artists Xoan Baltar and La Legra Negra from Spain first showed the way on Flickr, and Patricio Villarroel in Paris has shown us thousands of ways since. Famed artist David Hockney in the UK and Jorge Colombo in the US brought a huge amount of international media attention to the concept of art made on an iPhone.

When the iPad was introduced, iPhone artists went crazy. With a surface eight times larger and apps optimized for this powerful device, this was a whole new ball game. The app "Brushes" provided the tools painters needed from the very beginning and still does, but "SketchBook Pro" has made great strides in the past few years, with "ArtRage", "ArtStudio", "Layers", "Inspire", "Procreate", "PaintBook", and others in everyone's toolbox. Some apps are favored over others by different artists, each choosing apps based on a personal comfort level, but all are extraordinary tools when placed in the right hands.

In this section you will learn how traditional artists from all over the world approach painting on mobile devices. You will learn their tools of choice, their methods, and their inspirations. If you are a traditional artist, you will come away with a greater understanding of the various ways you can translate your existing skill set to creating art on these devices.

Painters will paint with anything, as art history has proven over and over again. They also are among the first to adapt to new technology or new ways of thinking. They are visual philosophers who comment on the world around them or on the human condition. They embrace new technology, but with a deep respect for the old. The diversity of the art in this section is a testament to the deep chord struck into the core of humanity by these devices created by Apple. Freed from the constraints of the studio or the desktop, artists, with the help of app developers, are creating a new kind of visual communication. The work is spontaneous yet serious, accessible and down to earth. Then the artwork is uploaded and self-published simultaneously to the entire planet Earth.

Pear

BY CORLISS BLAKELY
Artist
Vermont, USA

Established artist and seventh-generation Vermonter, Corliss paints still life and Vermont landscapes in a classically realistic style.

Corliss received her formal art training in Boston. While there she studied at Vesper George Art School and the Museum School of Fine Art.

Corliss Blakely has translated her expertise in oils to the iPhone, and using the app "Brushes", teaches us the subtleties in creating her luminous still lifes.

I start with a dark background, then paint using a transparent wash in the foreground. The pear is just blocked in, so I wasn't concerned about the shape or color. This approach to painting on an iPhone or an iPad is no different than one would use when painting in oils.

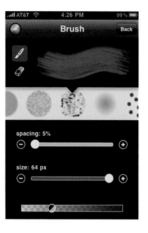

I start to paint the shape of the pear using transparent brush strokes.

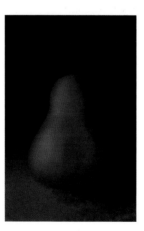

As you see, the pear has taken on a different shape. Next, I build up the painting by using transparent color and large brushes. I can use the eraser to clean up the edges when adding an airbrush effect.

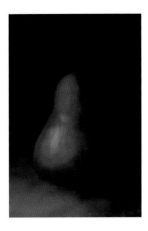

This is the blending stage. The skin of the pear has been softened and evened out. Now I begin adding the highlights and shadows.

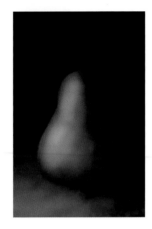

Time to play with more color. I love painting pears … each one has such a personality. I keep layering in transparent color because it's these subtle variations of color and light that give us the sense of realism. It is these subtleties that bring life to a "still life". I add strokes of lighter and darker shades of color to define the light source. Now I can see the real shape begin to emerge.

Just using two layers to create this piece so far, I wanted to capture the reflection so I added another layer.

Finishing the painting. This is when I concentrate on subtle lighting details, the soft light and the reflection of the pear. By using transparent soft brush strokes I have captured the essence of this pear, and its simple elegant beauty.

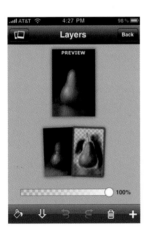

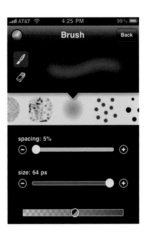

Mobile devices have opened up a whole new world for artists. It is the canvas that anyone can create on and send out to a worldwide audience with a click. I've always felt fortunate to be an artist, to wake up every morning and be excited to go to work … Wherever I am, at home, traveling, teaching art in Nicaragua or sitting at our cottage on Butler Island in Lake Champlain, my studio is with me.

White Cupboard

BY CORLISS BLAKELY
Artist
Vermont, USA

A master at traditional oils, a master at mobile art, Corliss Blakely demonstrates a still life captured on many layers.

Painted in "ArtStudio".

STEP 1

The first layer of the painting was the cupboard. By painting different shades on multiple layers with the preserve transparency option turned on, I was able to paint in the fine detail of the wood-grain. I went about this like an oil by glazing color and brush strokes to capture the patina of the grain.

STEP 2

The knobs were done on a separate layer. I used the airbrush to achieve the shine.

I describe my style as Traditional Realism. I'm a professional artist, internationally recognized for my work in several media, including watercolor, oil, and egg tempera. My paintings hang in collections around the world. But painting on mobile devices is like magic … It's hard to go back into the studio and paint oils.

STEP 3

Zooming in allows me to paint the smallest detail, like the chips and cracks in the cupboard's wood seen at right. Each brush can be custom-made so every stroke is exactly what you want.

TIP I used the airbrush eraser at a low opacity and gently painted the leaves so the stems, which had been painted first, would show through in a very natural way.

I love that my iPad paintings look like my oils. Painting in oils, you might spend days waiting for the layer to dry before you could paint again, and now the creative process is unimpeded. The iPad and my favorite app "ArtStudio" allow my paintings to come to life measured in minutes and hours instead of days and weeks. You can shut off layers, zoom in and concentrate on the smallest details, all with multiple undos.

"ArtStudio" is a full-featured app that has an amazing amount of features and painting controls. I suggest before you can fully appreciate this tutorial, whether a beginner or expert, you spend twenty minutes exploring this app's features.

STEP 4

Once I finished the knob, I started painting the vase and flowers on separate layers with the vase on top. By using the airbrush eraser on the vase, I can reveal the background gradually to simulate looking through glass.

This actual piece of lace I painted was made by my Great, Great Aunt Jenny in the 1890s, right here in Vermont.

I was born and I still live in Vermont. I grew up on a family farm and my mother had an antique shop. I started painting at an early age.

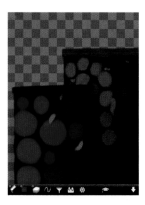

STEP 5

I started painting in the jars with basic shapes and then used the spray paint to make them come to life.

TIP The order you paint these elements doesn't matter as long as your highlights and shadows are consistent. Since each is on its own layer, you can re-order the layers to create the most pleasing composition while you paint and when you're finished.

Mobile devices have given me the freedom to paint anywhere. It has changed my life. I find that, now, I carry both devices with me all the time and it makes me a better artist. There are times when you see something or a thought comes to your mind and you think, "I would like to paint that ..." Well, now it's possible to start creating at that moment. No studio, paints, brushes, turpentine, rags, canvases, pens, paper or pencil, just my iPad ... How perfect is that!

It gets better! I love the fact that with one click, the whole world can see my latest efforts. I was one of the first people in Vermont to have a website, so I'm used to having my paintings out there. Visit me on www.ipadpaintings.com.

STEP 6

I finished the highlights on the jars and flower vase using the spray brush with low opacity and added a new layer for the lace. I drew in the outline and filled in the shape with a solid color. I then added a darker value for the shadow

STEP 7

I softened the shadow with the spray brush, then I used the pencil eraser to cut out the design in the lace. Zooming in, I outlined the opening with a lighter color, to mimic the look of embroidery.

STEP 8

I took out the black background to check and see if I had to make any changes. I softened the edges of the flowers to blend them in. One of the hardest thing for artists is to know when the painting is finished. I make all the layers visible, step back, take a careful look and say, "OK, that's it," sign it, done.

The Journey's End

BY THIERRY SCHIEL

Film Director, Artist, Animator, Illustrator
Duchy of Luxembourg

Director Thierry Schiel describes his technical process in creating this piece using the layers feature, and details in lighting. This is a clear example of the axiom in art that it's not the tool but the artist's creativity and raw talent that will ultimately shine through.

My interest in drawing evolved into animation and I appreciated much of the work of Disney, Don Bluth, and many French feature films as well. I studied at the Gobelin Animation School in Paris, during which time I discovered a world of fascinating short films and graduated to become an animator. Now, it seems I have always wanted to be a film-maker.

PICTURE 1—ROUGH SKETCH

For this illustration, created in the app "Brushes", I am looking for a concept that uses the layers feature of the app as much as possible, in order to emphasize depth of field. A scene with a strong foreground would be ideal. The sketch is done with the smallest brush at a medium opacity and is placed on its own layer.

PICTURE 3—COLOR STEP 2

The color for the background is now set and works well with the characters. I use large brushes with a low opacity to color the sky and land masses. Using brush strokes that are a little more precise, I rough in, then refine, the mid- and foreground elements.

PICTURE 2—COLOR STEP 1

I separate the coloring onto three different layers, keeping the sketch on a fourth layer, placed at the top of the stack. Layer 1: background; layer 2: the rocks in the middle; layer 3: foreground with bridge and characters. At this stage the colors of the background feel wrong, and I change

them for a different palette of tones. Layers are great for this. Because the background is on its own layer, nothing else gets disturbed, no need to change a line on the characters. The decisions I make here about the light source will determine how everything is painted from now on.

As a child, I was strongly influenced by Belgian comics artists like Franquin, Hergé, Peyo, and Morris, and I learned to draw by copying them. Later, as a teenager, my main influences were the French comics artists of the "Métal Hurlant" era, Giraud/Moebius, Méziaire, Bilal, Schuiten, Hermann (Belgian artists), Caza and, of course, da Vinci, Michelangelo, Vermeer, Rembrandt, Degas, Monet, Turner, John Singer Sargent, and so many others.

PICTURE 5—FINAL ART

What remains to do now is the final detailing for the characters. I improve them a lot by adding more contrast and a stronger light source coming from the holo-map the girl is holding and the staff of the bridge troll. Some final detailing on the top branches of the tree and in the foreground flora completes the piece.

My main interest, though, was in creating stories and characters that could have their own life on the big screen. To do so, I became producer and director of two feature films, Tristan and Isolde *and* Renart the Fox *(aka:* The Adventures of Renny the Fox*). The latter won several jury awards in various international festivals and both were screened in theaters around the world. All my films are done in 3D on "3ds Max".*

For me, iPhone and iPad art is in its infancy and there's always art to be made with these apps, any time, anywhere! That's the real beauty of it: art is finally mobile again. Another great aspect of it is the sense of community that has emerged from this new artform.

PICTURE 4

Now I finish the background and work on the middle layer with the towers and buildings, always keeping an eye on the global lighting picture. This consistency is key to placement of highlights and shadows that work.

I discovered that, for more spontaneous creation, the iPhone is a fantastically versatile tool. The iPad and quality of apps then take the medium to a whole new level. I started painting on the phone with the app "Colors!", then "Brushes" and "Layers". I now use the app "Inspire" most often for its great blending feature and "SketchBook Pro" for its high resolution, incredible line and superb set of tools.

PVB
2009

Ridiculous Room

BY PATRICIO VILLARROEL
Artist, Musician, Teacher
Paris, France

iPhone / iPad art master Patricio Villarroel works with multiple apps and finds a new way to construct or deconstruct another batch of abstract images every day. The next few pages detail how he sparks a visual idea, moves images through different apps, and winds up in some wonderful, magical place.

STEP 1

I begin this tutorial by playing in the app "Artisan". This abstract art generator has controls for speed, size, shape, color, and transparency that allow you to create an infinite number of variations. Do a screenshot on the iPhone to save your favorite to the camera roll. I chose this one to work with as the background for the piece.

To paint is to make music with my eyes, I paint with them, not with my finger.

STEP 2

I import the background to the app "NPtR", and combining the techniques "two finger quick" and "one finger slow" use the square tool to reveal sections of our background. Save this to the camera roll.

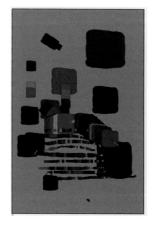

STEP 3

Open the background in the app "Brushes", and create two other layers to place on top as shown. I make our top layer active (highlighted in blue), and paint the floor with an opaque brown shade.

this room would have to be my room
there seems to be a video camera in it,
I don't know what to do
the light is peaceful the classical picture in
*   the wall is one*
I made 3 centuries before
How will I rest?

STEP 4

While leaving the layers in this order, I select the middle layer to make it active, and paint selected areas like the lamp and candle and start some outlining using a small white brush. Take the opacity level of this whole layer down to 50 percent to create subtle variations in overlapping areas of the piece.

STEP 5

I finish outlining the piece on the top layer now, and do a final adjustment of the transparency level of the middle layer. Finally, I sign the piece, save it to my camera roll and post it to Flickr.

autobiography (23)

BY PATRICIO VILLARROEL
Artist, Musician, Teacher
Paris, France

Patricio Villarroel takes us step by step through this graphic composition, from its rough pencil-drawing beginning to a most elegant ending.

STEP 1

Graphite 9B is my way of saying, "pencil drawing on paper". Using my iPhone and the app "Genius Scan", I photographed the drawing, adjusted the perspective and saved it to my camera roll. I opened it in the app "Photogene" to adjust the contrast.

STEP 2

I opened the drawing in the app "ArtRage" to place the image on a textured background, established the colors of the piece and then saved it.

STEP 3

Next, I opened the drawing in the app "GrungetasticHD" and after experimenting with the various settings and borders, fell in love with this one and saved it to the camera roll.

My father was a professor of mathematics and made pencil drawings during his youth. My mother was a French teacher and played the piano by ear without formal music education, so it makes sense that I'm in Paris now, teaching music to young musicians, and I create art on mobile devices.

I have been drawing since I can remember and studied classical drawing and painting (pastel). My first exhibition was in 1973, drawings in Indian ink at the Latin American Center in Paris. Twenty years later, I began creating digital paintings on my Mac and, for the past four years, have exhibited my mobile digital art in a dozen exhibitions worldwide.

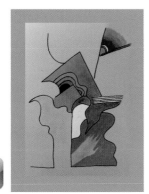

STEP 4

Finally, I settled into the app "Brushes" to create my composite and finish painting. The first layer is the saved image from Step 2, resized down to about 80 percent.

STEP 5

Still in "Brushes", I placed the image from Step 3 over the drawing as a new layer at 50 percent opacity, letting the grunge show through and creating a great border.

STEP 6

On a separate layer, but still placed below the grunge layer, I finished the piece by painting areas in gold and a dull teal color. I signed the piece, saved it, and posted it to my Flickr photostream.

My favorite painters are Kandinsky, Bacon, Miró, Picasso, and Alechinsky. I improvise music from scratch most of the time, and I do the same in painting: I draw with my eyes and make music with my ears.

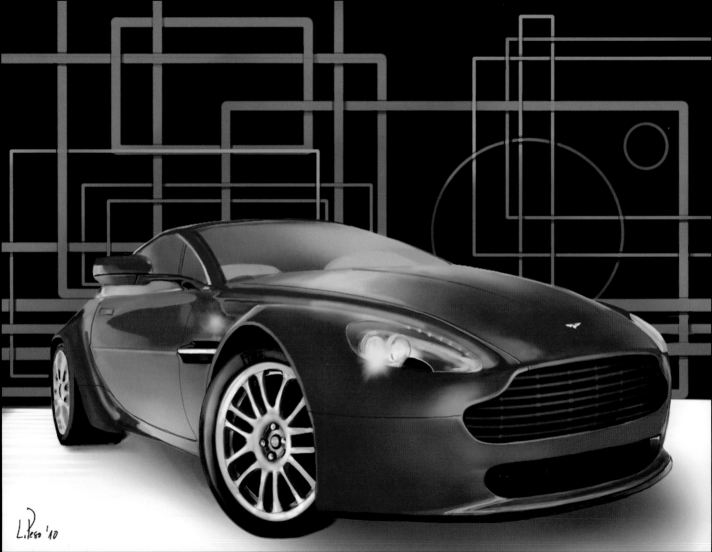

Aston Martin

LUIS PESO
Artist, Teacher
Granada, Spain

Master mobile artist Luis Peso trains his eye on a beautiful car and shows us why the iPad is his current tool of choice. Using the app "SketchBook Pro", this tutorial takes us into the details of his creation.

Painting on the iPad is as enjoyable as it is on the iPhone, but it also gives us more really useful tools to help us achieve great results, as I'll show you next.

FINGERPAINTING AN ASTON MARTIN WITH "SKETCHBOOK PRO FOR IPAD"

STEP 1

The main difference, of course, is the bigger screen. I made this rough sketch without the need of a zoom, while on the iPhone you must constantly zoom in and out to set every element in place.

STEP 2

Here's another great "SketchBook" feature you can enjoy while using the iPad: the layers' blending modes. As I made the rough sketch, I wanted to start adding color, to help visualize the composition. On the iPhone, I had to add a layer and apply color over the sketch guide; with the iPad, I can set the new layer to Multiply and another one to Screen so I can add a dark (and light) base without affecting the sketch.

Color Layer #1 Set to Multiply

Color Layer #2 Set to Screen

STEP 3

Working with the right mirror, where the tones are so evident, allows me to create the tonal palette I'll sample from for the rest of the painting, making it more compact.

Once I went to England, visiting a friend, and I saw a Ferrari 360 in front of the hotel. I was freaking out but my friend told me:"If you like that you're going to love this," and this Aston Martin appeared—the most beautiful automotive design I've ever seen in my life. I fell in love with its curves, its gentle but sportscar lines, its beautiful woodwork. I can tell you, the Ferrari looked like a Fiat next to this car. This is my tribute to its beauty.

Below, we see the same palette as it looks expanded, after painting the whole car.

STEP 4

"Sketchbook Pro" includes another great feature that we missed on "SketchBook Mobile", the shape tool. I use it for the background and for the radiator of this Aston Martin:

> Add an oval, move it until it fits in the right position.
> Duplicate it, move the duplicate to the right position and merge these two layers.
> Duplicate this resulting layer and again move it into position.
> Merge again, duplicate, and keep doing this until you're done.
> Then delete the rest of the circles (green marks) and you'll have a great radiator.

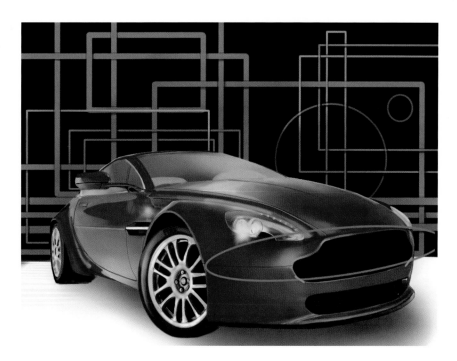

STEP 5

The bigger screen of the iPad, combined with the 2,500 percent zoom in "SketchBook Pro", allows us to work the details in a very comfortable way. "SketchBook Pro for iPad" was designed to function on this device with a screen eight times larger than the iPhone, so obviously it's easier to work this big. You spend a lot less time zooming in and out while working, but when you do need to zoom in on details, your abilities to create are extended to a new realm.

STEP 6

This version of "SketchBook Pro for iPad" also allows you to block transparent pixels, which means that you will paint only over previously painted pixels, not outside them. Use this to add lights and shadows to the radiator, and the beautiful highlights this distinctive automobile should have, to finish the piece.

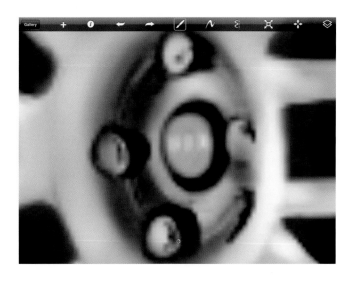

Mythological Satyr

BY BARBARA ARIANNA RIPEPI
Artist, Web Designer, Writer
Milan, Italy

Barbara Ripepi's experience with traditional media and the digital arts has migrated to mobile devices with elegant line drawings and sensitive portraiture.

The pictures I create with the iPhone or iPad reflect my style of traditional painting, drawing and digital illustration.

To realize *Satyr* I have started from a pencil sketch realized on a notebook usually used to draw user interfaces for iPhone (Notepod, http://notepod.net).

On the same layer I have started to perfect the line, working a lot with the zoom and refining the excesses with an eraser. In a few cases, the eraser turns out to be even more important than the brush to obtain an acceptable level of precision.

I photograph my pencil sketch to bring it into my iPhone and then open the sketch in the app "Brushes".

In "Brushes" I have left a white background layer for areas of light and on a new layer I have sketched out the image using a basic brush with a very low percentage of transparency.

The zoom allows for greater detail. Working with the eraser can improve the work, for example thinning uneven sections.

The artists I love the most: Egon Schiele, Dalì, Joe Sorren, Mark Ryden … In general I like Surrealism and Pop art.

I am only using the basic design as a guide. The design evolves through multiple layers that are merged when the work is satisfactory.

I was born and live in Milan, Italy. I studied traditional art and over the years I started concentrating on digital art, landing in the world of web design. I am a freelance web designer and I work in the communication field as well: I also contribute to a few Italian magazines as a journalist.

I have left the background coloring separate from the foreground, but maintaining an average percentage of transparency for the color of the figure to utilize the background for a few tones of the satyr's face.

"Brushes" allows the creation of up to four layers: to shade, I have created two layers, to be united later in one single layer, together with the original pencil. Layers allow you to refine the design by isolating the parts on which you are working. They are also useful when working with transparency. I have used different kind of brushes and varied the transparency a great deal to obtain the intended effect.

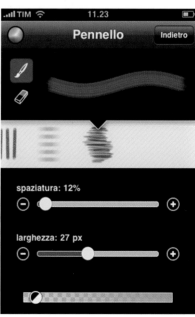

Hotel Tango

BY BENJAMIN RABE
Artist, Web Designer
Hamburg, Germany

Benjamin Rabe describes the technical process and the thought process involved in his artwork Hotel Tango. Using minimal amounts of color and minimal visual elements, the work manages to have maximum emotional impact.

For tonal clarity, I often start in black and white; I can always add colors later. I started by making two bold strokes using brush no. 3 in "Brushes" to get rid of the blank canvas.

I just started to define some space and an object.

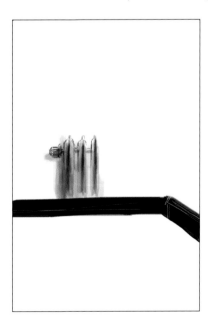

The radiator was molded out of the white using the soft black brush at 15 percent opacity. The outlines were defined using a 1 px brush at 70 percent opacity.

BENJAMIN RABE

iPhone Expressionist

I usually block the basic figure in with a dark color, then, using the eraser, subtract small areas to define the form. I go back and forth with solid color and the eraser until I've got a good silhouette to build upon.

TIP This is a typical "Brushes" technique that maintains visual consistency as all brush strokes have the same user-defined characteristics. It is not used universally or exclusively, but in this case to great effect.

By adding some simple details, our figure is now smoking and talking on his cellphone.

I created the shadow with a black brush at 80 percent opacity, then used the same brush as an eraser.

I made my first digital painting in the 1980s on an Atari 600xl in ASCII-Code when I was fifteen. After some studies in mathematics and physics I turned to web designing in the 1990s, bridging the gap between visual design and coding HTML/CSS.

My personal influences are: Loriot, Don Martin, Sergio Arragones, Caravaggio, Veronese, Hopper, and Turner. But my iPhone and iPad art is more illustrative than picturesque, more influenced by comics than by the Old Masters. I try to tell little stories.

Like digital photography, painting on the iPhone or iPad is almost instantaneous in two ways: creating the art, then getting feedback via Flickr and other social networks. The main thresholds which kept me from painting—costs, space, and time—have been lowered so deep I've painted more than 300 pieces this year. It was maybe thirty in my whole life before this new paradigm.

To create a muted color, I created a blue layer at 10 percent transparency and erased the white areas. This yielded a subtle color effect. I added smoke by painting grey and broke it up with the eraser. Details to the wall were added with black opaque strokes for balance.

Out of curiosity, I painted the background out with blue that I sampled from the wall and some black strokes in the upper right to change the location. Now we're free to put our figure wherever we want.

To finish the piece, I added some comic book great Will Eisner-style background that looks like a faint drawing in the upper left, and roughed up all the black areas using a fine multi-bristle eraser. The telephone cord, painted using a 4 px brush in a tell-tale curlicue brush stroke, settled this final image into a time way back when everyone smoked and no one had heard of a cellphone.

Figure 6

BY ROBERT DAWSON
Web Developer, Artist,
iPhoneographer
California, USA

(Had he moved to southern California, his abbreviated residential history would have served as a palindromic signifier of *weltanschauung*.)

I was born and bred in Alabama, attended Memphis College of Art, and majored in Graphic Design. There, I became one with the web and have worked full-time as a web developer ever since. Now, I live near, and work in, San Francisco.

The following steps describe the creation of this iPad painting. Due to the unidirectional flow of spacetime, these steps cannot be repeated, although imitation is theoretically possible ... However, these steps may prove linguistically instructive to the touchscreen artist requiring descriptive inspiration for his or her own published work.

0a Walk into a coffee shop.

0b Order a real cup of coffee. Yes, a real coffee, but I mean a real cup. Save a tree as well as your own aesthetic integrity.

0c With coffee in hand, add your preferred adornments, take a seat, and place the glistening elixir in front of you.

0d Grab an iOS device. For this painting, I chose my iPad.

1a Open a painting app. Here, I chose "Brushes" for iPad.

1b Pick a brush, any brush.

1c Squint and find three colors, representing the darkest, midrange, and lightest areas, respectively.

1d Block in each color from dark to light, filling the entire space.

1e Smile. You've just nailed your composition.

2 Frown. You forgot a color.

ROBERT DAWSON

Homage to Coffee and Its Cups

3a Start adding detail.

3b Take a moment to thank the incredibly selfless cup before you that is holding your scaldingly scrumptious coffee, acknowledging that you are both earthly vessels and that if you were made of porous clay, you would absorb the liquid into your own body without compunction.

Requirements:

> Must like coffee.

> Must respect coffee and coffee cups.

> Must have coffee.

> Must paint coffee before consuming it.

> Must like cold coffee.

4a Prove your thankfulness to the inanimate container by blocking in the coffee, adding vivid color to what was before a dreary scene.

4b Apologize to the cup for calling it dreary. You didn't mean it. It's just that surely you can both agree that coffee is exquisite.

5 Scribble in more detail and some floorboards. Don't airbrush it or blend edges between values, pretending to be Leonardo painting the Mona Lisa. Don't insult the subject by denying it its life-affirming energy. Scribble. Let each stroke exude exhilaration.

6a Conclude your homage with a splash of contrasting purple color over the cup's previously dull shadow. This should make the cup feel better.

6b Now you can smile again.

I grew up painting with oils and acrylics, and still do. If the iPhone and iPad could provide smell and tactility and messiness, minus lead poisoning, I might give up traditional painting altogether. When I paint on mobile devices, I tend to do so naturalistically, by painting portraits and still lifes.

Having these mobile devices lets me quickly bring creative ideas to life. I love paper, but these devices are so much easier and more convenient for realizing flashes of creative insight. I tend to use them to capture momentary inspiration. For example, if I see a child yawning or maybe a tall building in downtown San Francisco with sunlight gleaming off one side, I will quickly grab my iPhone and take a picture. Other times, I'm inspired to paint a woman's hair in front of me on the train.

The ability to instantaneously publish art across the globe with one tap or click and then receive feedback in minutes is unbelievably unprecedented in the history of artistic creation. I consider myself so lucky to be alive today and try to make the most of this opportunity, exploring and breaking creative boundaries.

I am a cartoonist, and while I am quite conservative in that field (I mostly use a brush and ink) I must confess I often use computer tools to draw my color pictures, be they professional or not. I was never attracted by the drawing applications designed for the iPhone. The screen seemed too small for me, and even if I was surprised by what some artists could produce with it, I was never curious enough to give it a try. But the release of the iPad and its "large" screen turned everything upside-down! The iPad is like a true sketchbook. It lies on the corner of your desk and is operational in a few seconds; you can start a drawing then stop halfway to come back to it later with incredible ease and speed. It is really convenient to carry around, the picture quality and the color rendering are excellent and, best of all, the touch screen permits direct contact between your finger and the picture. This feels more natural and intuitive than the average graphic tablet.

A Day in the Country

BY MATHIEU REYNÈS
Artist, Cartoonist
Léon, France

Mathieu Reynès thought the iPhone was too small for consideration as a tool to make art, but is making up for lost time as he makes "Brushes" sing on his iPad.

STEP 1: THE BASIC SKETCH

As a rule, I start with a rough pencil sketch which I use as a starting point. More often than not, the final picture does not really look like my earliest sketch. The idea behind that picture was to contrast the size of the elements, to oppose what is small to what is large: a big sky and a small piece of land, a gigantic tree and a tiny car. I also felt like creating a very airy, Zen atmosphere.

STEP 2: THE BACKGROUND

I start with the sky. For this picture, it will define the general atmosphere, the light, the picture dynamics. I especially love drawing clouds, I find it relaxing … so I start with roughly positioning objects and placing their shadows. Thus I locate my light source. Then I define the horizon by placing a line for the ground. I add a few low-flying clouds and a light mist to add depth. I work on the details to make the clouds more precise and puffy.

STEP 3: THE TREE

Moving on to the tree, I position the objects: the trunk, boughs, and leaves. I work on several layers to have a variety of boughs and leaves (dark in the background and clearer in the foreground). Afterwards, using the rough sketch as reference, I give volume and detail by positioning shadows and clear lines. I want very dense foliage so I do not hesitate to create a very dark shadow zone. The tree has not been completed yet, but I prefer to move on now to the car and possibly to return to it later, to adjust the colors.

It's fun making art on the iPad because you're holding it in your hand as easily and lightly as a sketchbook. You can rotate it as it suits you, use it wherever and whenever you want.

The ability to manipulate the tools and features directly with your fingers really brings the digital device closer to traditional tools such as paper, pencils, and brushes.

For me, the iPad allows for more freedom and spontaneity in digital art. I make art not only at my desk, but on the train, comfortably on my couch, listening to music or in my garden in the shade of a very old oak …

STEP 4: THE CAR

As I did before, I place the objects and define the elements, then I add volume by placing shadows and light. The mist in the distance does not look contrasted enough to me, so I underline its presence by making it more yellow. This makes the picture somewhat warmer and provides an easy transition from the sky to the ground.

STEP 5: THE GROUND

I give volume to the ground by placing shadows and lights. I add more detail to the grass. Again, I use several layers to underline depth (dark hues in the background and clearer ones in the foreground). I make a few flowers grow, and presto! That's done the trick! The layer depicting the mist is placed on top of all the others, which therefore allows it to influence them all, giving depth to the picture at very little cost.

STEP 6: THE ROAD SIGN

The road sign was not on the initial rough sketch, but the idea blossomed as I was doing my coloring work. The drawing process remains the same: first objects, then details and light.

STEP 7

A few finishing touches to highlight some contrasts, and my picture is complete … for the time being!

I was born in Paris but spent all my childhood in Biarritz. I studied in Bordeaux and Angoulême and now live in the little village of Léon, because I can't live far from the ocean …

Mathieu Reynès **49**

Tango

BY NECOJITA
Artist
Kyoto, Japan

Necojita details his painting process and the importance of maintaining perspective and the direction of the light source to give even this representational piece a greater feeling of realism.

STEPS 1 AND 2

Using the app "Brushes", apply the colors with a large brush across the large blank screen. Use only dark colors for the foreground figures and a strong balance of background colors. It's important to establish a broad harmony of color and not worry about smaller details yet, since our goal, in the images below, is to block in two central figures, mother and child. I also rough in the purple Koi, or carp, in the background.

NECOJITA

Perspective and Light

STEPS 3 AND 4

I am aware that we are viewing the figures from a low angle based on where I have painted the horizon line. This perspective is important when drawing the skirts, the details in the faces, and the Koi, to get the feeling of it hanging in the sky. Create new colors while blending the colors in the sky. Get comfortable using a brush at a low level of transparency. Using a much smaller brush, I now add the facial details of our subjects and details in the clothes, and start to define our background Koi.

STEP 5

I add details to the purple Koi at a low transparency setting, which gives us the ability to add these details and blend the colors simultaneously. Adding white details at 20 percent looks like a lavender brush stroke on the purple Koi and keeps the colors unified.

STEP 6

I add two more Koi to the background to increase the feeling of depth.

STEP 7

By drawing in the clouds, I can clarify the direction of the light. The representation of reality requires the correct light from the background to the foreground figures of the mother and child. Be conscious of painting using subtle tones. Finalize the background details.

FINAL IMAGE

I used "Brushes Viewer" to generate a larger file size and cleaner images when printing.

"Tango" is a festival in May celebrating the growth of children. Koi are made of cloth and are used in the traditional Japanese custom of decorating the outside of the home.

Square 1

BY SAM TANG

Artist, Photographer, Musician, Writer, Inventor, Engineering Manager, Systems/Software/App R&D

Illinois, USA

Sam Tang has been making art on his iPhone since the day the iTunes app store opened. His approach to this new canvas is revealed using a simple yet capable, easy-to-master— and *free*—painting app as he embarks on a family mission.

"Dad, can you help us make a CD?" The new musical trio which included my son Sammy on drums brainstormed and settled on "Square 1" as their "sick" namesake. Firing up my iPhone and the "iDoodle2 lite" app, I took a stab at a concept for their debut album destined for the Top 40.

STEP 1

Open the app "iDoodle2 lite". Before even thinking about the design, I set a bold tone using a bold color as our background. Tap "Menu", then select "Edit Background". Playing with the RGB color sliders, to mix together just the right amounts of red, green, and blue, I dialed in an electric blue, clicked done and it poured this beautiful blue all over the screen.

STEP 2

For strict straight lines, pick the line tool; I was going for a more organic look here so I selected the pen tool and let my fingers do the walking and painting, crookedness and all. Using a thin, white pen for more accuracy, I roughed in a 3D number 1.

STEP 3

Filling in some untouched background real estate, I coated the underlayer with a faint, weavy brick pattern to echo the square theme.

TIP Click "Tools" to decide between the pen, line, blob, flood, rectangle, oval, and eraser tools. These tools are obvious and even the blob tool has no learning curve. Experiment! Have fun!

STEP 4

I drew a 3D cube encircling the digit using a slightly larger black pen at a lower opacity.

Sam Tang's career in software engineering could and should be its own book. From working with the small team that invented Motorola Cellular Digital Messaging Protocol (Texting), to personally creating and demonstrating an i-phone prototype ten years before Apple's iPhone, to building a wiretap system for the Federal government after 9/11, Sam is a man of many talents.

STEP 5

Taking advantage of extra space near the top, I spelled things out, putting "SQUARE" in custom, squarish, and obviously hand-drawn type above the graphics.

TIP Try a hand-written font of your own design, as in this image, to add even more personality and memorability to your message. Custom text can reinforce your message and image among a sea of images with polished professional graphics and fonts.

STEP 6

I wanted to amp up the dynamic range and drama on the piece with a full range of values from pitch black to pure white. I started by adding a gray box around "SQUARE" and surrounded each letter with square white boxes. I then added a dramatic, white, glowing, orby circle around the cube for maximum contrast in values and shapes. Next, to add even more depth and a little bit of framing between the orb and the rectangular edges of the digital canvas, I painted in some cryptic, deep black corner pieces.

STEP 7

Play with the light! You are painting with light, not paint. A thick brush, with white, almost transparent paint, was used to create a nearly clear bubble around the central "1". With multiple touches, the highlight at two o'clock was gradually added. Finally, to make the bubble "pop", a big, black, nearly transparent brush was used in layers to add a dark, contrasting vignette to finalize the piece.

You may find a hint of Monet mimicry in some of my work, as I've had many of his paintings (OK, prints) hanging on my walls to look at, study, and enjoy every day. There may be a touch of Dalí and bizarre, dreamlike subject matter thrown in as well, along with some M.C. Escher, whose technical precision combined with creativity I still marvel at today.

Joining groups of like-minded souls will also treat you to a daily influx of new and exciting paintings and experiments. Flickr (www.flickr.com/photos/samdtang) is the way to go because it plugs you into a world of other creatives, many willing to give constructive and otherwise helpful comments on your work. Feedback from other artists is invaluable.

I cranked out this concept in minutes, but unfortunately there's one thing faster than operating on internet time, and that is the disintegration of teen bands. So, alas, the design awaits, on standby, for the next incarnation of this boy band—or should I say, "Square 2.0"?

On the Shoulders of Giants

BY MATTHEW WATKINS
Artist, Illustrator
Bari, Italy

Along with co-contributor Benjamin Rabe, Matthew runs the iPhone/iPad art blog, www.fingerpainted.it, where his work, as you will see below, is as inspirational as his source. Here, he shows us how he incorporates his drawings and sketches into his mobile devices for further exploration using the app "Brushes".

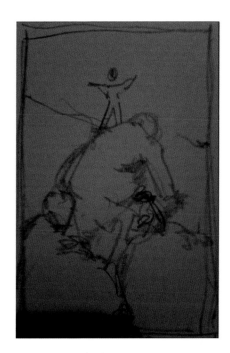

To integrate drawings with mobile devices, take a rough picture of the drawing using the iPhone or iPad camera. The quality of the photo doesn't matter, as it's there for reference only. This is a moleskin drawing of mine used for this piece.

If the photo is dark and blurry that can be a plus, creating soft tones, greys and purples, that you can draw into.

One of the tricky things about doing a watercolor is that you have to keep preserving the white space till the end. With iPhone or iPads this is not a problem, as you can create white space whenever you want.

MATTHEW WATKINS

Sir Isaac Newton and Mobile Digital Art

Using the photo of the moleskin drawing as the base sketch, I start painting by putting the white space back in.

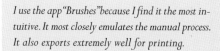

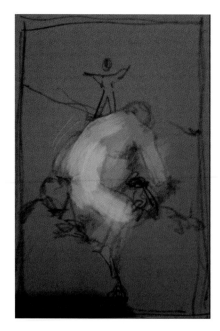

Once I have blocked in the composition, it's time to experiment with areas of color. I begin to develop the highlights and shadows.

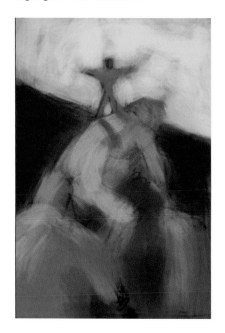

I increase the contrast of the piece by pumping up the dark areas and going for a more intense yellow.

My list of influences is long: Caravaggio, Rembrandt, Klimt, Schiele, Hopper, Bacon, Andrew Wyeth, Lucian Freud, Rauschenberg, Rothko, H.R. Giger, and illustrators from N.C. Wyeth to Frazetta, Bernie Fuchs, and Brad Holland.

The Flickr photo-sharing network has been a revelation. It's addictive. It's part of the democratization of the artistic process. You don't have to hang in a gallery or be published in a magazine to get your message out there. Art has never been so accessible. You make a picture, you upload it to the social networks. Five minutes later you are discussing it. It's awesome . . .

At this point all brush strokes should be very transparent, so that all additions are subtle, requiring multiple overlapping strokes.

This picture was drawn on camera for the Italian RAI TV network. They have a three-minute segment in their Art News *show where they film an artist creating a work of art. It was a great honor for me and indicative of the interest surrounding mobile art. This drawing was complicated by the fact that they were asking questions while I painted and I'm not used to that. They were very patient while they were filming me, and just when they thought we were done I decided that the piece needed some pinks ...*

Giants

I have used this drawing a couple of times in my business presentations. It's an ironic take of mine on Sir Isaac Newton's famous quote, "If I have seen further, it is because I have stood on the shoulders of giants." A Swedish physicist recently asked to use it for the cover of his thesis. Like him, I find this an inspirational concept. Newton was a giant: he saw further than others. He understood the importance of the contribution of the giants before him. If I pause to think about the enormous technological advances that have made mobile digital art possible, I understand that they have been the fruit of generations of great minds working together. The little guy on the top is not a giant, it's me, or another mobile artist, or anyone who has been able to see further than he might have had it not been for the generations of giants and their hard work. And the view is wonderful, it really is.

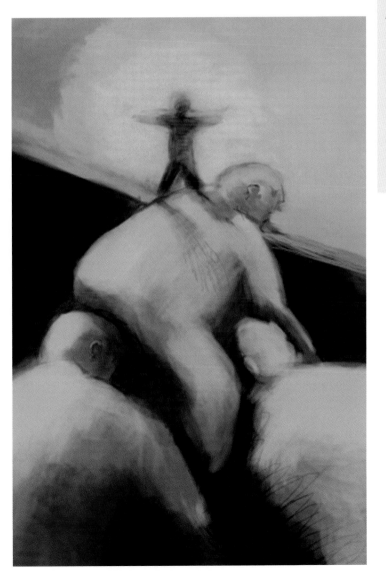

The small character at the top is backlit, so to heighten this effect I put some yellow edges around him, and fade out the arms with some light transparent strokes.

To finish it off, I added some "lens flare" by taking the largest brush and making small circles at different levels of transparency. And then I added back in some details on the top figure for definition and clarity. Finally, 1 px yellow and black brush strokes create depth and definition and 3 px yellow brush for my initials and the date.

Steampunk Mona

BY MATTHEW WATKINS
Artist, Illustrator
Bari, Italy

Matthew Watkins has been a moving force in mobile art with his site www.fingerpainted.it, co-developed with Benjamin Rabe, his work on Flickr, and exhibits of his iPhone and iPad art in the real world.

La Gioconda is arguably the most famous and iconic painting in the world. Leonardo da Vinci was a visionary who has perhaps known no equal. Paying homage to the great man, and a score of Dadaists, Surrealists, and Pop artists along the way, seemed like a fun way to take my iPad for a spin. A theme in my recent work has been destructuring portraits, breaking them into smaller pieces as if they had been bolted together à la steampunk. This is what I had in mind for Mona.

I start with a good-quality scan of the original.

After opening the image in the app "Brushes for iPad", I began gridding out the shapes, following the contours. Dividing her into plates.

Using colors sampled from the great man, I started blocking out the plates, and adding bevels and highlights. I like to work with transparent layers, not the micro-thin glazes or *sfumato* that Leonardo used, but not solid color either.

I began to focus on the background, essentially doodling forms and buildings over the landscape with loose attention to the shapes below. I am pretty sure, though, that it was not the *Città del Futuro* that Leonardo envisaged.

The combination of the iPad's physical size and the ability to zoom into the artwork takes the artist's attention to details to a whole new level.

I added two mischievous bunnies and a robot in chains.

Mona's arms and hands got the steam-punk treatment.

Next I started filling in the shapes while mostly being faithful to the color palette of the great man.

Leonardo da Vinci is said to have started La Gioconda *in 1503 and finished it only shortly before he died in 1519. It only took me a couple of hours to steampunk it. But I couldn't stop wondering as I painted ... what would the great man have done with an iPad?*

Some finishing touches on that enigmatic smile.

The miracle of iPhone painting using the app "Brushes" is that you get to work on a small screen and still output in high res. The iPad gives you a seemingly infinite canvas in comparison and even higher output resolution. Your imagination is the only limit.

I find myself developing quick concepts on the iPhone and then detailing them on the iPad.

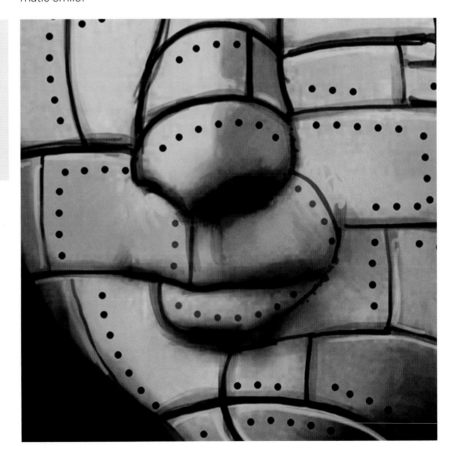

Marine Biology

BY DAN HOFFMAN
Artist, Creative Strategist
New Jersey, USA

Dan Hoffman is a freelance creative strategist working in interactive media. He lives in South Orange, NJ, USA. More of his mobile art can be found on Flickr and in the iCreated iPhone app and gallery.

The thing I love most about mobile painting is the feeling of creative freedom. Part of that freedom is that I can paint where I want, when I want—my iPad and painting apps give me the portability of a sketchbook, but with the full color palette and painterly effects of the studio. For me, freedom also means being able to make it up as I go along—to start with a loose concept and fill in the details—or even make major changes in direction as the painting process sparks new ideas.

Marine Biology started with a pretty loose, almost abstract concept. I envisioned a rather foggy, mysterious seaside landscape, and a female figure standing on a rocky jetty extending away into the distance. (The painting's title came at the end of the process, after improvisation added some elements that weren't even remotely part of the original concept.) Since I was much clearer on the atmospherics than on the specifics of the figure, I decided to start by blocking in the sea, sky, and jetty. Knowing I might want to change direction with any of these elements later, I painted each one on a separate layer.

THE BLOCK-IN OF THE BACKGROUND LANDSCAPE

The ocean, jetty, clouds, and sunlight are each on a separate layer. The first major "improv" was to the sky. I started to feel I wanted to see the sun peeking out of the gloom. I started a new layer, and I liked that bright splash of sunlight so much that I started to paint some blue sky around it. Eventually, the atmospherics changed from fog and gloom to a dramatic sky with the sun breaking out through receding storm clouds.

Having redone the sky, I needed to rework the sea. Starting on a new layer, I painted over the grayer, murkier original with more bright yellow-greens, as the sunlight shone through the peaks of breakers and the shallows alongside the jetty.

DAN HOFFMAN

Marine Biology

"Procreate", the app used to paint Marine Biology, *is great for this kind of "improv" approach, because it supports up to sixteen painting layers (most apps support a maximum of only six). That's great for trying out different ideas on different layers—different background tones, atmospheres, or even major changes to the main subject of the painting. If you change your mind, you delete the layer; if you're not quite sure, you can hide that layer while you try something else. Aside from its layers, I find "Procreate" to have a great selection of brushes and a smoothing/blending mode that's the best I've found in any app.*

At this point, I was pretty happy with the landscape (and skyscape), so it was time to start in on the central figure standing on the jetty. I started by blocking in a woman in a full-length skirt and hooded top, a mysterious figure covered from head to toe by clothing. But I realized pretty quickly that this figure didn't quite mesh, thematically, with the brighter, more dynamic direction I had taken with the landscape. She looked like someone bracing for a storm that had already passed.

As I began rethinking the figure, I started wondering what she was doing out there on the jetty in the first place. The concept began to shift from a mysterious but passive wanderer to someone more actively engaged in exploring the seaside environment. I hid the layer with the hooded figure and started blocking in my new character, shedding the hood and long skirt for rugged jeans and boots and a funky top. Details of the character continued to evolve through improvisation on multiple layers.

EVOLUTION OF A CHARACTER

Layers were turned on and off, added and deleted repeatedly as I worked through different ideas.

The birds, whale, and nautilus were added near the end of the painting process. Having created my seaside explorer, it seemed her explorations should be rewarded by adding some aquatic creatures to the environment. The nautilus held by the character, the seabirds flying overhead and the whale sounding in the background were all layered additions put in near the end of the work.

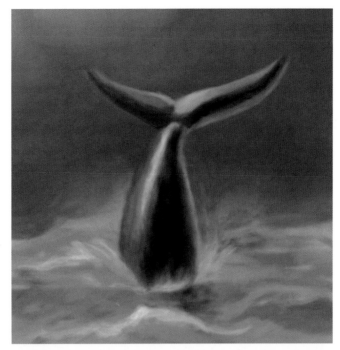

The Death of a Dictator

BY GABRIEL PALACIOS BADILLO

Artist
Azcapotzalco, Mexico

"SketchBook Pro", "Pixlr-o-matic", "Tile Wallpaper", "Camera+".

INSPIRATION

When I paint simple digital brush strokes, improvisation makes them more complex and colorful as I go along. Unfortunately there are times when those strokes produce nothing original to satisfy me or to let me create something visually interesting. In these cases of low creative energy, I don't look at other painters' work for fear of becoming a copycat. I try to consult photographs in a search for images that will provide me with some meaning. One of my favorite and recurring sources of inspiration is the gallery of the Library of Congress which is posted on Flickr (http://www.flickr.com/people/library_of_congress/). In this gallery you can find material from different photographers and eras, free of copyright but with important historical value.

Mother Jones. Bain News Service, publisher (between ca. 1910 and ca. 1915).

Samuel Gompers on stand. Federal Commission on Industrial Relations, NYC. Photoprint, 1915 (Bain Coll.) (LOC).

SELECTION

I usually choose four or five pictures that are visually interesting, specifically selecting ones with some peculiarity in the people in the photo: their clothes, the posture of the body, the expression on the face, or a way of using some object. This selection is done quickly, without analysis, a mere glance.

Once you've selected the photographs and placed them side by side, try to find some relationship. This relationship is invented by me, of course, an attempt to develop a narrative in which you can view your found photos as part of a story worth telling.

DESIGN

Recently, during the process of selecting photographs I found the image of a man sitting on a podium, reviewing some documents. He seemed to hold the power to make decisions on important issues.

The other picture I found was of an older woman, dressed elegantly. Her appearance reminded me of the way death is represented in Mexico: a finely dressed woman with a skull for a head. I noticed that the woman carried some documents in her hands. At the time, unconsciously, I established a fictional relationship between the two pictures: What if both documents were the same picture? What if they had the same message? It occurred to me that the woman (representing death) could be taking a dictator a list of people who were about to die. Among the names on the list would be the dictator's.

I placed the reference pictures on two layers.

I cut out the characters and put them in position, in accordance with my composition.

I added another layer on top to draw on, using the photo as a reference.

I added a bottom layer with a texture and an intermediate layer for adding color.

TIPS

1 Use photos for reference only, not to avoid drawing. Avoid painting on photos without using your imagination.

2 Use as many layers as necessary. Put the dark layers at the bottom, bright ones on top. Adjust light and shadows in the appropriate layer.

3 If a layer isn't working, simply delete it and start a new one.

4 Do not paint the textures of the objects in the scene. Make separate textures and apply them when you need to.

5 Put a textured layer below the layer you want texturize and gently erase (with 2 percent opacity). You can see how the texture appears on objects in a more stylized way instead of being simply painted in.

TEXTURE OF CLOTHING

The screening was done by repeating the pattern with "Tile Wallpaper".

I imported one of the textures for the second layer. The purpose was to add texture to the dictator's clothes. Placing it on the first layer, I took the eraser tool, set the opacity to 2 percent and started to erase over the dictator's body. This action revealed the texture behind, on the second layer, as if I was painting over the surface. Once I finished his clothes, I merged both layers.

Once I finished painting, the image had shades of blue, a color that did not correspond with the drama of the moment I wanted to portray. Therefore I decided to apply color filters. I used the apps "Pixlr-o-matic" and "Camera+" (separately or together) to optimize the color, changing hues to add texture to give the painting a better look and to create atmosphere. With the "Camera+" app, I applied the Chromogenic filter to the image and saved it. This gave an ocher tint to all objects and textures, as well as a faint granular texture to disguise stroke imperfections and unify all the elements of the image. Then I opened "Pixlr-o-matic" and applied the Soft filter to shade the corners, getting a shadowy effect. The aim was to highlight the white paper and the very important message it contained.

Texture of the wall. Pattern: "SketchBook". Pattern repetition: "Tile Wallpaper".

Black and White Magic

BY DAVID STERN
New York, USA

David Stern's professional art career spans over three decades and his work is included in museums and private collections nationally and abroad. Here, in a few pages, he shares some art and some mobile art philosophy.

Drawing is the oldest discipline of the arts and the most direct. The material requirements are minimal, a mark-making tool and a surface to use it on. It does, however, require an enormous and complex effort in abstraction. According to paleontologists, our species developed this ability for abstraction almost 40,000 years ago.

Humankind achieved its first victory over individual life spans and time through drawing; the artifacts of the Paleolithic, like the cave drawings of Lascaux, still communicate to us the experiences of the dawn of our species. I use touch-screen devices to jot down my own experiences, leaving them in a "cyber-space cave", enjoying the thought that they might be still there hundreds of years from now.

I was born in Germany, immigrated to the US in 1994, live in NYC, studied at a studio school in Dortmund and at the Dusseldorf Academy, both in Germany, and have been a working artist for more than thirty years.

Drawing is a magical process and drawings can be magic objects. The simple fact that a few lines have the power to evoke images, memories, concepts, and emotions in the visual cortex of the creator and the viewer is magical.

This first page shows stages of an observational drawing I did on the iPhone in the subway and belongs to a series I call The Passengers.

STEP 1

A line takes on volume and makes space in a two-dimensional medium.

All the drawings in this chapter were done with the app "Zen Brush".

STEP 2

Sometimes, I feel lines are not enough to define the space the figure is situated in; here some shades of gray convey the idea of the platform and the dark tracks.

STEP 3

Adding a second figure changes the entire exercise into a more complex image with figures interacting in some way, opening new straits of meaning.

Drawing on touch-screen devices has liberated me from paper sketchbooks and allows me to take "notes" undetected in public. Some of these fast sketches inform later paintings. That's my own victory over time.

Some of these drawings are done more deliberately on the iPad and sometimes help clarify problems I encounter with my paintings.

This page shows stages of a drawing I did on the iPad, while working on a small series of paintings called Affections.

THE KISS

STEP 1

I stayed with the principal idea of the drawing throughout the entire process, which took about an hour, trying to solve the formal problems of two heads in interaction, kissing. The first two images show the beginning of the drawing; note that the second (male) head is still positioned behind the female head in a frontal way, without any perspective shortenings.

STEP 2

By continuing, I started to foreshorten the male head projecting out of the frame of the format. This adds a bit of dynamic and allows the viewer to get "sucked in" to the drawing. I also used the eraser on the app to "lighten" the drawing and give the few defining lines more prominence.

STEP 3

Finally, I added some gray shade in the negative space between the heads. This brings out the two principal forms of the heads, but also keeps the drawing ambiguous, creating independent forms which now dominate the heads.

I am a painter, so I made and still make paintings, drawings, and prints using a whole array of real materials in the real world. I added another medium by adopting the technology and using touch-screen devices to draw. I also work on several projects which include displays on LED screens, projections, and displays on dedicated websites.

My influences are very widespread, over more than five centuries; my work is informed by artists ranging from Rembrandt to de Kooning.

I find it absolutely liberating to have an unlimited sketchpad with me at all times. It helps to be spontaneous, almost casually observing my surroundings without drawing any attention to myself. Drawing on the devices also allows one the luxury of saving a version of a drawing and then developing it further without losing the original, which is exhilarating.

Some of the pros of mobile art are instantaneous worldwide publication, the possibility of collaboration with other artists, the freedom from physical materials, and the possibility of producing different versions of the same drawing in various states.

Before painting on these mobile devices, I just created on paper (painting, pastel, pencil . . .). Now, I draw a lot more often. Having the camera handy is critically important in dealing with moment-to-moment inspiration.

STEP 1

I start with a rough sketch and composition, with a small mid-opacity black brush. It's important to keep things simple at first to see the painting as a whole.

STEP 2

I only get into details once I'm satisfied with the composition.

Granny Gore

BY CÉDRIC PHILIPPE
Artist, Student
Paris, France

Granny Gore is built from scratch using the app "Brushes", as this talented artist reveals his methodology and thought processes.

CÉDRIC PHILIPPE
Mobile Digital Artist Personified

STEP 3

Now the hardest part: color blocking. The farther away things are, the more desaturated I paint them. Complementary colors with a bit of blue are used for shadows and very saturated colors for lit areas. You must already be able to feel the depth, the light, and the atmosphere at the end of it.

STEP 4

Once my colors are roughed in, I develop different areas of the composition, remembering, most importantly, where my light source is—in this case, the fire in the belly of Granny Gore.

STEP 5

Finally, polishing. From the background to the foreground I overpaint each bush, each creature, mostly with a mid-opacity fourth brush, always sticking to my color keys.

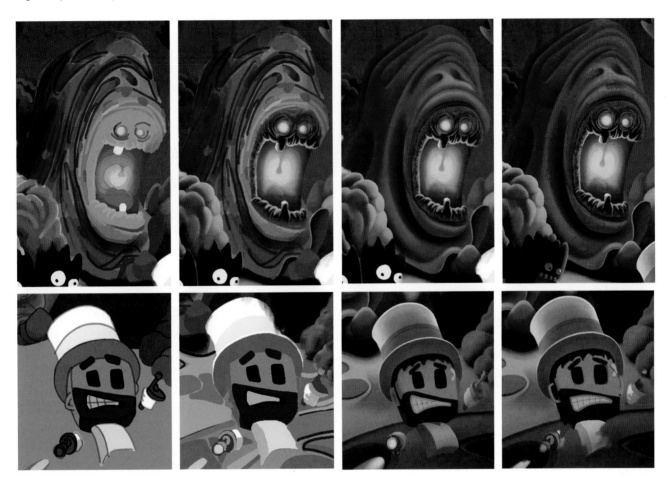

This painting is based on the tiny universe Timo Vihola created for the iPhone game "Minigore", whose hero is here about to be smashed by a raging Grandma.

Fingerpainting on the iPad has a drawback: it will never have the taste of traditional media. But being able to share your art online as soon as it's done and to export the whole painting process of each piece really makes it worthwhile.

I'm currently studying in Paris. I share my finger-paintings on Flickr, iCreated, and on my website (http://cedricphilippe.blogspot.com). Having that mobile artist community at my fingertips is a fantastic experience!

STEP 1

I started out in "ArtRage" and began painting a gray undercoat layer in a slate gray/green using the widest roller brush.

STEP 2

I continued with using a combination of the roller brush, oil brush, and even watercolor brush to create a pattern in gold, orange/red, and black on the second layer.

Love for 3 or more Oranges

HELENE GOLDBERG
Psychologist, Artist, Writer, Musician
California, USA

Thousands of iPhone and iPad paintings later, Helene Goldberg displays an incredibly smooth and sophisticated path to abstract heaven.

HELENE GOLDBERG

Abstract Calm

The main reason the first part is in "ArtRage" is that there are some subtle shadings and textures that I couldn't have gotten with "Brushes". My feeling was to just create a pattern in orange and blue that was asymmetrical and that I could transform in "Brushes".

STEP 3

In the third layer I added an orange circle using the roller brush.

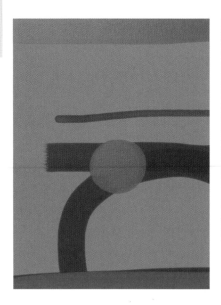

I do many abstracts because I love Abstract Expressionism for its energy, pure color, and composition. I love to listen to music (generally Beethoven, Bach, or Coltrane) while painting on my iPad or iPhone.

On my seventieth birthday, I got a call from the events planner at the San Francisco Flagship Apple store asking me to do a solo presentation of my art because I was "cutting edge". My paintings have been in many exhibits of mobile art in the past three years and I'm thrilled to be included in this book.

Today I am primarily working with "ArtRage" and "Brushes", though I love to experiment with different apps and to push their limits.

The "Brushes" Flickr group has become a major part of my life. I wake up in the morning eager to see my friends' paintings and to enjoy their reaction to mine. I feel incredibly lucky for the support and encouragement the group offers and I'm amazed that such a solitary endeavor is shared with so many people. Until now, I think only the most successful artists had their work exhibited, but thousands of people have viewed my and all my friends' mobile digital artwork on Flickr and all kinds of social sites that we post our art to these days.

From the time I first discovered painting, when I was sixteen, in a social studies textbook, I was drawn to the Expressionists and abstract artists most of all. It started with Picasso and Matisse and then I fell in love with the Fauvists and the German/Austrian Expressionists. I love Chagall for his colors and Schiele for his delicate lines. Later I saw paintings by Kline, Rothko, Motherwell, Miró, Kandinsky, and de Kooning, and was enthralled. I think you can see these influences in my paintings.

STEP 4

I added some more orange and blue/gray to unify the composition and saved it to my camera roll.

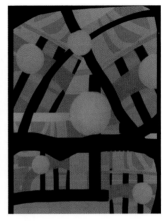

5a Two duplicates of the original moved around.

5b Duplicated again and arranged in reverse.

5c Image with black lines pulling the composition together.

STEP 5

In "Brushes" I used different layers to create new effects. To begin with, I duplicated the main image four times, pinched it down, and used the + icon, located in the Layers palette, to move it around. That way I could use my own painting to create a collage composition. I placed the second layer with the now four images over the original and then opened a new layer. In that layer, I painted the black lines that suggest a tent frame.

STEP 6

Final image with shading: I used the airbrush, painting with a soft, semi-transparent brush to successfully imply shadows and dimension.

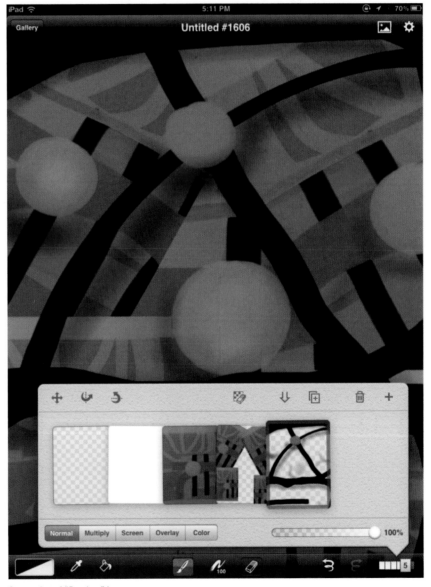

Screenshot of "Brushes" layers.

Meat Store in Cairo

BY JOSE ANDRÉS GUIJARRO PONCE
Obstetrician, Gynecologist,
Medical Researcher, Writer,
Artist
Cuenca, Spain

Jose Andrés Guijarro Ponce, known in the iPhone/iPad art world as "La Legra Negra", shares his precise steps to creating a mobile digital modern masterpiece.

When working with "Brushes", using a lot of transparent colors, it is important to choose a background color before starting work. I choose a shade to bear a resemblance to a neon light inside the store, a cold and desaturated green.

Usually working with a quick pencil-like sketch, I start with some fine lines at a 50 percent opacity without worrying about whether the curves are angular or the strokes are overlapping. I complete the sketch with black opaque fine lines.

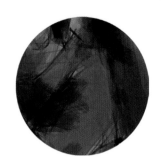

I apply color tones starting with the lightest and darkest colors at an 80 percent opacity and then with intermediate shades of color by applying layers of fairly transparent color (20 percent opacity) to the existing tones in each area for realism and shading.

I started creating art in adolescence with cartooning, and after I had tried several media, such as oil, acrylic, and pyrography, I used mostly watercolor. I think this experience is evident in my approach to painting on my iPhone and iPad. I've also created illustrations for advertising, so I have experience with "Photoshop", vector-based software, and 3D applications, and bring that sensibility to my mobile art.

My professional job is as a doctor of obstetrics and gynecology and I also work in research for assisted reproduction. I have recently been the medical director of a public hospital. I am the founder of published journals, the most recent being **Memoria**, *a magazine about general history, published monthly in Spain.*

I modify the base color slightly, with big strokes of very transparent (5 percent opacity) color, giving a little blue to the interior and yellow to the outside light. At this point, I start to shape the final strokes, starting with the background. Now my brush strokes are more precise and opaque, and I sample color from each area for more definitive strokes. It is time to incorporate fine lines for details of light, shadows, and some color hue using a brush with a high opacity.

Five-year-old twins leave me little time to pursue painting. So the possibility of a drawing program in my pocket on my iPhone is an idea that came down from heaven.

I continue the same procedure for the foreground, focusing somewhat more on the details to finalize this piece.

It can be especially difficult when people's faces are not portraits but a small part of an image, because small deviations in brush strokes can create a dramatic change in facial expression. You may need multiple touches to get the desired results.

It is very important to take the small details into account, in that the image you see on your iPhone/iPod is very different from the details you can see after exporting a large image file to the "Brushes" viewer on your Mac.

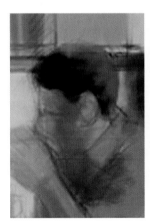  

01
21
HUNTINGTON 09

Ocean Liquor

BY STÉPHANE KARDOS
Art Director, Artist
California, USA

This talented artist will demonstrate why painting in the dark is a unique place for your iPhone or iPad to shine. Using the app "Brushes" and a glowing backlit display, he can build this cityscape at night as clear as day.

I recently moved to California and really love the light here. The LA sunsets are gorgeous, but painting a sunset live with paints is very challenging. The light goes away quickly, and it's very difficult to see the colors on your palette as the sun goes down. This is where the iPhone or iPad comes in handy. It gives you the opportunity to paint a sunset live. Because of the backlit display and the possibility it offers, I've also painted a lot of neon signs around LA, and among them this Ocean Liquor sign that I'll use as an example, to show you the different stages of this mobile painting, using the app "Brushes".

This is a screenshot of the brush I use all the time. I like it because it gives a more "organic" feel to the final painting, less digital. I don't go around the various settings too much when I paint, for the simple reason that I want to be fast. The whole idea is to create the complete image while the light is just right. So I use only one kind of brush, vary the size for details toward the end of a painting, and use transparency a bit, and that's about it. I don't even use the layers as they weren't available when I started to use "Brushes" back in 2008, and I got used to painting without them. I just go straight to the point, building my painting from the bottom up.

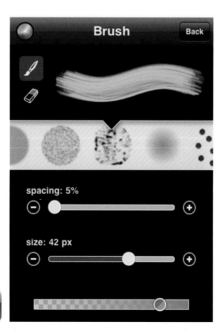

STÉPHANE KARDOS

Neon at Night

I start with a dark blue color and, using very large brush strokes, create the background for the piece. It's the very last glow left in the sky before nightfall.

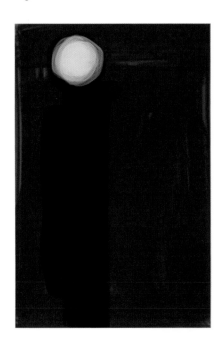

In the interest of speed, I break down the visual elements into abstract patterns. Right now, it's only about shapes, colors, and composition. Notice that I establish the position of the lightest and darkest compositional elements early in the process.

Once I lay down the main shape of the sign, I block in the neon lights. By adding some highlights, I get the neon sign effect, and emphasize the contrast.

I am originally from France, where I studied animation and illustration. I currently live in Los Angeles, California, where I work as an art director for Walt Disney.

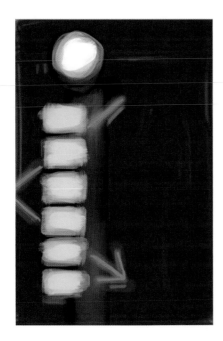

Next, by adding some additional highlights, I build up the neon sign effect, and each new light source pops against the night-time sky.

Then come the letters, which I do by hand but in an orderly fashion, plus the very important bit of green neon light at the bottom of the composition. It adds a nice reflection under the yellow sign, and another level of depth.

I add the writing inside the top round sign by zooming into the image and painting with the smallest brush size, then slightly darken the inside of the red "liquor" letters with a larger brush and a slightly darker red tone for a more realistic effect.

Finally, I use very large brush strokes to darken the top part of the sky, which makes the neon sign pop out of the composition. Then I add the red light reflection under the top round sign for more depth and volume. Finish up with a couple of stars in the sky on this chilly January night in LA. And *voila! Fini!*

Solar Flare Highlights

BY DEBORAH MCMILLION NERING
Artist
Arizona, USA

This talented artist creates this piece in the app "SketchBook Pro for iPad", and shows us how using layers for compositing helps add dimension to our fiery portrait.

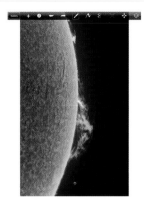

STEP 1
Begin by importing a photograph of the sun.

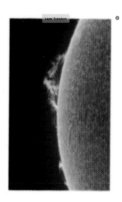

STEP 2
Rotate and resize it to fill the canvas. I'll use this as a guide to paint the solar flare for the background.

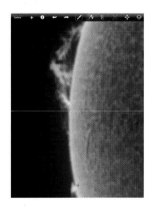

STEP 3
Duplicate this layer so we have two suns. Erase the background black of the upper layer and duplicate it again. Now there are three layers.

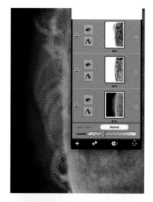

STEP 4

I fill the layer with textures and use the eraser to "draw" holes in the top layer. Creating holes lets the detail in lower layers peek through, creating a sense of depth and complexity.

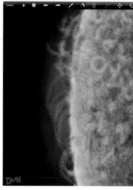

STEP 6

After creating a third texture on the lowest layer, I make the upper layers semi-transparent. The resulting blend of transparent areas and semi-transparent brush strokes combine to create the finished effect.

STEP 7

I start the figure in a new layer by blocking in with an opaque brush. Base contours and shadows are added using a slightly transparent, neutral color with a slightly feathered brush.

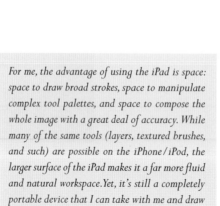

For me, the advantage of using the iPad is space: space to draw broad strokes, space to manipulate complex tool palettes, and space to compose the whole image with a great deal of accuracy. While many of the same tools (layers, textured brushes, and such) are possible on the iPhone/iPod, the larger surface of the iPad makes it a far more fluid and natural workspace. Yet, it's still a completely portable device that I can take with me and draw anywhere.

STEP 5

I use various textured brushes to paint contrasting patterns on the middle layer.

STEP 10

I begin by duplicating the layer. Starting in the lower layer, I add dark, soft tones using a thick feathered brush.

STEP 12

A very powerful feature of "Sketch-Book Pro" is the Preserve Transparency feature, not available on the iPhone version. It allows you to draw in a layer without "painting over" the transparent portion of that layer.

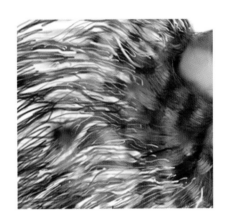

STEP 8

Using progressively finer, more transparent brushes, I slowly build up the detail, highlights, and shading. Repeatedly going over the same area with progressively more transparent and softer brush strokes gives the sense of blending and glazing that you would achieve in oils.

STEP 11

Working in the upper layer, I start using streaky brushes to create hair-like texture. I then alternately use the eraser to create holes in between strands, while adding successively finer detail and streaks. Towards the end, I add highlights and accents.

This feature allows you to touch up, tone, blend, and highlight the edges of figures and fine detail (like hair) without obscuring the layers underneath.

STEP 13

With all layers visible, add initials on a separate layer to finalize the piece, and save it to the camera roll.

STEP 9

With the figure's face nearly complete, I now want to develop her hair. I do this using multiple layers to create complexity and a sense of depth, much the way it was done for the background.

Taylor Swift

BY SALVADOR NAVARRO
Artist
California, USA

Salvador Navarro, a self-taught caricature artist, has always loved to draw, but for some strange reason always felt inclined to do this particular type of portrait. Here he takes us through the steps to his obvious success.

Trained with pencil on paper … and after a long affair with caricature art, I tried digital painting ("Photoshop", "Painter") but always came back to my pencil … then the iPod Touch came along, then the iPad, and the rest is history. I'm now addicted to this fingerpainting craze!

In the app "Brushes", on a clean layer, I start by jotting down the general location and shapes of the subject, using the pencil tool at very low opacity. Save the result to the camera roll.

I open the sketch in the app "Sketch-Book Mobile", which allows me to transform or rotate this layer as needed to fit all the features I want to include. I use this app just to transform the layer, save it to the camera roll, and open it up in the app "Brushes". Once the proportions feel right, I lower the opacity of the layer to 20 percent and create a new layer on top to refine the pencil drawing. I'm trying to capture as much detail as necessary before I begin to paint. I start to get a feel for the values and colors using a wide translucent brush, adding some base color for the next step.

TIP Notice how the eventual highlights to the piece are blocked in early, on the chin, cheek, and forehead.

To add color to this layer, I start with a wide, opaque brush and choose a medium tone for the skin. It's easier to add highlights and shadows later. I do the same for the hair, eyes, and other features.

I continue building up the blocks of color, then switch to the airbrush tool and, using a large, very low opacity brush, start applying layers of the colors that are already on the canvas that I sample using the eyedropper tool.

It's just great to be able to create when inspiration strikes, sometimes in odd places at odd times!

I open the last saved version from "Brushes" back into "SketchBook Mobile" to transform the layer and create some space around the face to add much more hair. Save it to the camera roll and open it for the last time in "Brushes".

I truly believe every time one looks at an art manifestation some of the information is processed and stored by the brain. Then, when it is time to create, that information is filtered and intermixed with one's personal style and comes out a little different with every new piece.

I continue this process using the airbrush tool, smoothing and blending the previously applied rough strokes. Now I'm choosing colors that are going to increase the impact of the final image, in this case the reds and golds, and place them subtly in key spots, sometimes switching between layers. It is this constant back and forth observation between my reference and my device that allows me to capture the slightest variations.

I decide to add a dark background to make the hair pop, so we just add a new layer and fill it with a reddish brown.

I move on to my least favorite part, the hair, which includes eyebrows and eyelashes done with the smallest brush. Create a new layer for this

purpose and handle it the same way as the skin, painting with subtle variations in color, but at a high opacity.

I finish the painting by choosing a spot for my signature, always on a separate layer in case it needs revision.

If I'm working in "Brushes" I export the image to "SketchBook Mobile", and after saving it to the gallery, email it to myself. This way, I can open it in "Photoshop" on my Mac and do a little tweaking of contrast and color saturation before printing … nothing major … but the images look a lot better on the iPod Touch screen than they do on the computer monitor, so I adjust the image to make it as close as possible to the original file.

The Whale and the Octopus

BY BORJA AGUADO AIZPUN
Artist, Motion Graphic Designer
Bilbao, Spain

This precise tutorial examines working in the app "Layers" and takes us on an amazing underwater journey.

I've always start my drawings in the same way: with a soft, very small brush. For me, the main point is to not be afraid of the white canvas. Frame and perspective are key points.

BORJA AGUADO AIZPUN

The Whale and the Octopus

The next step is to choose the color palette. I make a new transparent layer under the scribble layer and then I paint with a middle-sized, textured, and slightly transparent brush.

In the next stage, I slightly adjust some details of the subject and choose what kind of light the scene has. In this scene the characters are underwater so all colors have to be slightly tinted with the scene's general tone.

The brush I use in this stage mainly depends on what area I'm working in, but is usually a small, highly transparent brush. This way, if I need darker shadows, I apply more than one stroke. Once we finished the shadows, we'll repeat the same process again with the highlights.

Next step: I fill the background layer with color. This is when I give the octopus his color and sharpen his details. With a big, dark brush, I loosely draw the area that later, with more detail, will become the coral.

With a small eraser, I create highlights on the main characters. This is the first step to getting detail in the drawing. When you are drawing an illustration, sometimes as important as what you draw is what you erase.

Now the only thing that's left to do is the details. Adjust highlights and shadows, draw the teeth of the whale, the octopus's suckers, the coral's details, the octopus's head shades ... once you've got the general drawing, adding this kind of detail is the easiest part.

I am in many groups on Flickr. Some are for illustration and other art on the iPhone. It's awesome, it's fun, the people are friendly, and others' comments encourage me to continue drawing. I think there are many people who don't know how important the internet is for promoting and connecting artists.

I have lots of influences. My favorite classical artist is Leonardo, and the most modern, H.R. Giger. And then there's Hopper, Pollock, Picasso ...

Rapturous Cyclops

BY KARA JANSSON KOVACEV
Artist, Illustrator, Graphic
Designer
New York, USA

Kara shows us how to build a 3D puppet with an app that mimics molded clay. Then she'll bring that rough clay to life with her portraiture painting expertise in the app "Brushes".

I received a BFA in painting and printmaking from the University of Massachusetts at Amherst in 1992. My work includes painting, printmaking, puppetry, toy theater, installations, costume design, animation, web design, illustration, and now ... iPhone and iPad art.

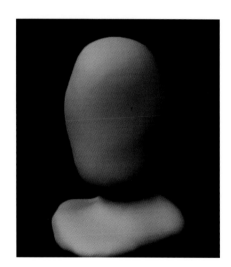

I start off by modeling a head using the app "Sculpt-Master 3D". "SculptMaster" has only a few basic tools: adding, carving, and smoothing. There is no ability to stretch, warp, or texturize as in a typical 3D modeling program, and there is no mesh to make subtle alterations. The experience is similar to modeling with clay. I start off creating a few general spheres that are modeled roughly, with my finger, to create the basic shape of a head.

Then I use a Pogo stylus to do the more delicate carving and shaping of the facial features. The stylus allows me to work on very small sections of the piece without my finger obscuring the working area.

The size and tool constraints of "SculptMaster" don't allow for very fine detail, so I model the figures to the point where they can be transferred to the app "Brushes" without losing too much of the clay-like quality. "SculptMaster" allows you to rotate your object 360 degrees, so I select the frontal angle to use and save a copy to the camera roll.

I then import the image into "Brushes" and rough in the details, often extending the body or adding to the background.

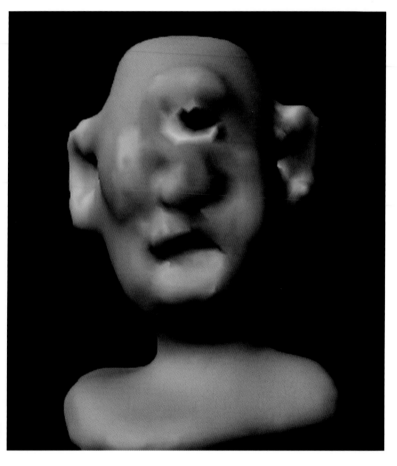

My personal influences are 15th–17th century Dutch painting, symbolism, medicine, programmable electronics, mythology, early Puritan America, space, and the future.

I often mash up the past and future in my work, and like the way these creatures—stodgy and stuck in some distant time—are propelled to the present on the pixelated glass screen.

I refine the features, especially the eye, and then concentrate on flesh tones. These characters evolve in the creative process, but I did have French symbolist painter Odilon Redon's gentle cyclops in mind and maybe a portrait by the 17th century Dutch painter Frans Hals.

The cyclops symbol occurred to me while drawing on my iPhone—I imagine it a contemporary cyclops of sorts with its singular illuminated eye. At first, I intended the virtual puppets to be mock-ups for my real puppets, or as animation vehicles. While I have used them for those purposes, they started to take on a life of their own and I now think of them as stand-alone pieces. The real puppets take many hours of modeling and stitching—I usually make only four or five in the course of a year, whereas these "digital puppets" can be created on my daily ride on the train. I started using "Brushes" in April 2009 and "SculptMaster" in November 2009 and have made more than 200 drawings and thirty iPhone puppets. While not a replacement for my other work, it has been wonderful to have this little pocket studio with me at all times to capture fleeting ideas.

FINAL IMAGE

I created this piece in three layers: the "SculptMaster" layer, the background layer, and the top retouching layer. I usually redraw a majority of the image on the retouching layer, leaving only a small amount of the "SculptMaster" file visible. I start with a thin brush at full opacity and draw outlines on the top layer and highlight important details like the eyes and nostrils, then add subtle shading with a larger brush and less opacity to liven up the skin tone. I finalize the piece by working the reflective details and highlights in the eye, and giving our cyclops a few teeth.

I wanted the cyclops to seem contemplative and dreamy so I chose a more open layout. I was thinking of Dutch portrait painting with the black background. The contradiction of this naked beast, smiling gently in a pose once reserved for nobility, appealed to me.

Just wait until mother

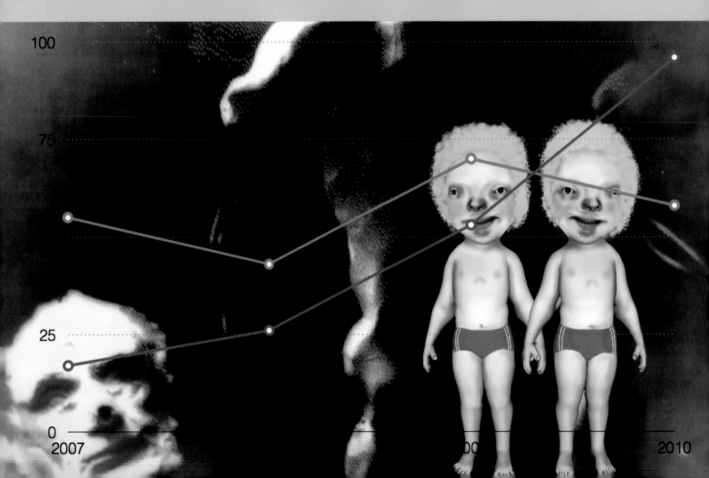

Collaboration on All Levels

BY CRAIG NEWSOM
Artist, Professor
Illinois, USA

Digital and traditional methods do not need to be pigeonholed or separated in the artist's toolbox.

Craig is an educator, born and raised in Iowa with a BA in English, a BFA in Painting from the University of Northern Iowa, and an MFA in Sculpture from the University of Chicago. Craig is currently an Assistant Art Professor at Blackburn College in Carlinville, IL.

Collaborative Artwork

BY KARA JANSSON KOVACEV
Artist, Illustrator, Graphic Designer
New York, USA

Kara is an artist with multiple disciplines and is particularly well versed in mobile digital art and the many ways today's artists need to interact with the web and each other. Her personal chapter precedes this one.

This piece is a good example of combining work from different apps as well as using apps in unexpected ways. In addition, it's a combination of traditional and digital approaches to creating art.

I have always been interested in collaboration on all levels of artmaking. There is a subjugation of the ego and an inherent critique system built into the fabric of the collaborative process. I have collaborated with several artists on different projects with varying levels of success in the past. Success always hinges on a very careful and respectful combining of two separate aesthetic systems. In 2011, I began collaborating with Kara Jansson Kovacev, who is the author of the previous chapter in this book. After a few projects, we realized our methods and ideas were so closely linked that we decided to direct the bulk of our artistic efforts toward collaboration. We call ourselves Coalfather Industries (coalfather.com), which is, of course, an obscure hybrid reference to capitalism and various naming conventions for the devil in several Nathaniel Hawthorne works of fiction. Since we live a long distance from each other we had to work out a number of issues with our workflow.

It would seem, at least on the surface, that the iPhone and iPad are uniquely suited toward long-distance teamwork. However, some important steps need to be followed to ensure smooth communication and file exchange between whatever number of individuals are working on a project. There are two major online file-sharing and storage sites: "Dropbox" and "Box.com". Both of these sites have corresponding iOS apps.

The "Dropbox" app is a good deal more robust and useful than the "Box.com" app. A lot of apps have built in "Dropbox" support. So, if you are sharing a folder with someone on "Dropbox", you can upload a native file to that folder and the other person will have direct access to it. As of this writing, that is not possible in a direct way with "Box.com". Both aforementioned apps are free. There are also paid apps you can use to add more function to these free accounts. One such app is "iFiles". It allows for multiple "Dropbox" and "Box.com" accounts as well as linkages to sites like Flickr, Facebook, Google Docs, and interaction with WebDav and FTP services. Using an app like "iFiles" as a hub for file exchange is an efficient way of dealing with sending images, video, and documents back and forth.

The freedom of having this device with you at all times means that ideas can be instantaneously made manifest and then transformed.

"Just wait until mother" is a slide from a longer "Keynote" presentation we eventually exported to video. This particular video, Family Time, has been screened in England, France, and Carbondale, Illinois. We often use "Keynote" as a place to work out narratives as well as produce individual works and permutations of pieces that can eventually be exported to video from a computer.

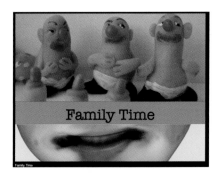  

Additional Screenshots from our *Family Time* Video.

My personal influences are William Blake, Francisco Goya, Aleksandr Rodchenko, William Kentridge, the Bauhaus, Philip K. Dick, Fyodor Dostoevsky, every Sid and Marty Krofft production ever made, Gorecki, Stars of the Lid, and Lawrence Welk. They reveal themselves in my mobile digital art in bleak and maniacal ways …

I make amalgamations of imagined locations and individuals and video using a combination of the apps "SketchBook Pro", "Keynote", "123D Sculpt", "Pixlr-o-matic", "StopMotion Recorder", "Harmony", "ReelDirector", "iMovie", "Splice", "GarageBand", and "miniSynth".

Original Photo.

The background image is a scan of a photo I developed in the darkroom from a contact print of a digital negative printed on a transparency. This was downloaded from my Flickr photostream and placed directly into the iPad.

The twin personages are 123D meditations on the Infant of Prague Kara crafted on her iPad.

The grid and the text are all constructed inside of "Keynote". The great thing about working in "Keynote" collaboratively is that elements can be placed in separate slides and then moved around like actors on a stage. It's possible, using the WebDAV setup inside of "Keynote", to export presentations directly from the app to an online file-sharing site. The finished piece, then, is a single slide from a longer "Keynote" presentation we exported to video.

It should be noted that both of these pieces were created using asynchronous collaboration techniques. Presently, there is a new app available called "Sketchshare". This app actually allows two or more artists to work on an image at exactly the same time. The tools are limited in this app—but the possibilities are staggering.

If you are considering collaborating with another artist using your mobile digital devices, set up a "Dropbox" or "Box.com" account. It works much better to have an entire account that is shared. Individual folders within accounts can be shared too, on a case-by-case basis. Once that is set up, get to know the exporting capabilities of the apps you are working with. Many of them do link directly to "Dropbox" folders. Some, like "Keynote", also support WebDAV or FTP export. Also, if you are combining images, get a handle on how those images are actually exported, i.e., jpg, tif, png, etc. The file type that handles transparency well is png, which will allow you to combine images without backgrounds. Finally, be ready to troubleshoot. Collaboration is gradually growing and expanding in the mobile digital art community. Hopefully such capabilities will be more prevalent among apps in the near future.

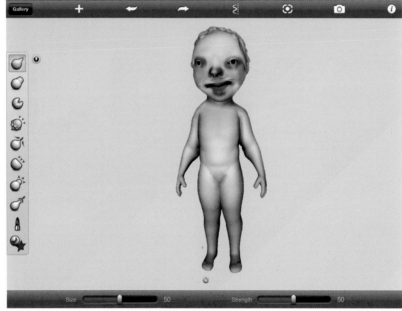

Kara's Screenshot from "123D Sculpt".

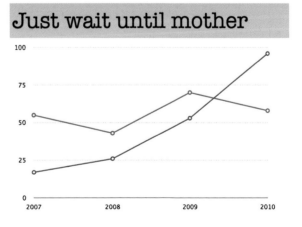

The Old Bridge of Mostar

BY ROBERTA KAPSALIS
Artist, Professor, Graphic
Designer
Mostar, Herzegovina

Using the app "Brushes", Roberta Kapsalis starts with a dark summer sky, and teaches us to fill the frame with beauty, depth, color, faith, and hope.

I was born in Sarajevo, Bosnia (exYugoslavia), but spent most of my life in Herzegovina. I graduated at the Academy of Fine Arts in Computer Graphics and have made a lot of computer art, but sometimes I work in classic mediums like pastel, acrylic, and graphic engravings. I have worked as a teacher both in a high school for the fine arts and the Academy, and am the main designer for all publications and new websites for our university. Graphic and web design is my daily job, but art will always be my focus.

Since I'm painting at night, I start with large, opaque strokes to create the dark blue background, and then a tan brush to rough in the composition.

Next, I define the horizon with details we see through the bridge, some foreground building details, the water below and its reflection.

ROBERTA KAPSALIS
Painting a Cityscape at Night

The old bridge of Mostar is made of stone, so during the day it's all grey. At night, there are large yellow lights surrounding it, which turns many of the stones to a golden hue yet leaves some stones grey in a beautiful patchwork.

To paint a proper starry night, I have to zoom in quite a bit. That way, using a very tiny brush, I can draw dots that will be softened later, to give the impression of distant stars. The addition of green foliage helps establish a vivid foreground and a link to the background.

iPhone and iPad painting is great because you can redo parts of the image over and over again until you are satisfied with the result. While I was painting the old bridge, the ambience of the sky and the light changed several times before the piece was finished, and these changes are expressed as very light washes of color, blended together to create atmosphere.

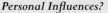

Photosharing groups like Flickr make me fall in love with computers all over again. These groups have become the best way to meet other artists, to hear their opinions and to get important feedback. I love this new way we communicate today and can't wait for the communications of tomorrow.

Personal Influences?

My computer art is influenced by Victor Vasarely. My iPhone art is different, influenced by Croatian artist Dimitrije Popović. My space works are inspired by Hubble telescope images …

Finishing touches include adding some deep reds, to make the distant hills more vibrant, warming up some of the window light and then, using very small opaque brushes, to paint in all fine details on the rooftops and the bridge.

In the town of Mostar, the famous 600-year-old bridge stands in the middle of the city and connects the two sides of the city, Christian and Muslim. During the war this bridge was destroyed, and it has since been rebuilt. I like to create beauty here, in the hopes that my art can shine a different light on this place called Mostar, and help heal the wounds of the past.

In 2010, this stamp was the world's first postage stamp officially published by a national post office (Hrvatska pošta Mostar) that was created on a mobile phone (iPhone). I painted the image in "Brushes", and it portrays the late priest Fra Slavko Barbarić, a very important humanitarian during the war, on the tenth anniversary of his death. My artwork was entered in a national contest, selected as the best painting and made into this stamp.

Mobile art is like liberation. I get ideas in the most unusual places. From now on, I can make sketches anywhere I want. That's real freedom!

Running into Colors

BY NINI TEVES LAPUZ
Visual Artist
California, USA

Painting in three apps might seem redundant to some, yet this artist teaches us the advantages she finds by doing just that, with some important lessons in transparency thrown in for good measure.

Photo 1 ("Layers")

I started the painting in the app "Layers" using some bold strokes at maximum opacity, then used the smudge tool, which "Layers" has with adjustable texture, size, and pressure, to blend the colors, achieving the effect seen in Photo 1. This step is saved to the camera roll.

Switching into the app "SketchBook Mobile" I imported the painting created in "Layers", added a top layer and painted on the blank canvas with an eraser. I continued this process to selectively reveal the painting done in "Layers". When I was satisfied with the result (Photo 2), the image was saved to the camera roll.

I love to use vivid colors and the emotions and movement an artwork could evoke. There is also the usual pantheon of artists, Van Gogh, Matisse, Renoir, Chagall, Cassatt, O'Keefe, and Kahlo, whose works still enchant me, as does the Japanese art form ukiyo-e or the floating world. The same evanescent and seemingly mundane but exquisite elements that attracted the Impressionists, I have begun to see. Childhood memories of idyllic scenes, genre paintings from coral and palm-fringed tropical islands, also serve as an infinite resource.

Photo 2 ("SketchBook Mobile").

The previous image was opened in the app "Brushes", and a transparent layer added on top of it. Using bold, opaque brush strokes with the eraser tool shaped as shown at right, I painted a group of lines running down almost the entire length of the canvas (Photo 3).

Photo 3 ("Brushes").

When I'm fingerpainting, I feel I am running into and engulfed by colors. With my works using the different painting apps, I am seeking the same epiphany Paul Klee had when he saw the intense light in sun-drenched Tunisia: "Color has taken possession of me; no longer do I have to chase after it, I know that it has hold of me forever. That is the significance of this blessed moment. Color and I are one. I am a painter."

If this were traditional art-making, it would be an assemblage, an arrangement of miscellaneous or found items. Simultaneously, the piece is rich with state-of-the-art multi-media capabilities.

By combining, re-ordering, and changing the level of transparency of individual layers, "Brushes" allows me to find a place that's just right to finalize the image above. It is such an absolute benefit to have layers functionality available in the three applications used to create this piece. "Brushes" gives the most fluency and vigor in showing the cumulative effects of each layer, and also has a slider that lets you adjust the opacity of each one. Alter-natively, or simultaneously, you can take advantage of the transparency functionality that is available in every shape and size of brush in "Brushes" and "SketchBook Mobile". Yet one more way to work with transparency is the ability to control the opacity of the eraser. Using the eraser in conjunction with layers allows so much deftness and confidence in expressing the most subtle or the most spirited ideas I may have at the moment.

Fast, Gestural Painting

BY BENOIT TOUBAB BAUDE
Painter, Illustrator
Lille, France

Benoit Toubab Baude has a visceral feeling about painting on mobile devices and shares the process in his stylistic portrait. The steps in this chapter are built for speed where brush strokes and color become intuitive and spontaneous.

I use the app "Inspire" for a more traditional painting with its many brushes and HD export; "Adobe Ideas" for its vector brush, extremely powerful when you have to switch between mobile devices and desktop; and in this tutorial, "Brushes" because it's my first love painting on the iPhone, for its ease of use and its great variety of tools.

I'm from Boulogne sur Mer, and now live in Lille in the north of France. My work is painting and illustration. I've had three years of formal art studies, but learned the most from friends, other artists, group discussions, and sharing art on the internet.

STEP 1

I always start with color before painting to work with color's contrast from the beginning. Here I start with the purple background. I can begin to place the head on the canvas with big strokes, I choose a warm skin tone to contrast with the cold, purple background.

My plan is to use these two colors and also use the many different tones that exist between them, to maintain a harmonious palette.

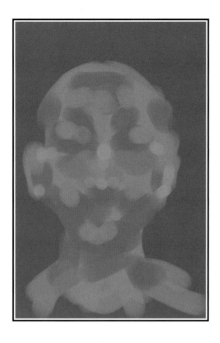 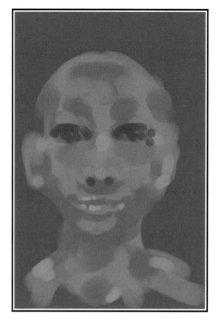 

STEP 2

I start to put the first mixed shades in place and play with combinations of these two colors to create the basic volume of the head.

Now I can paint with a lighter color to highlight different parts of the face, like the nose.

As I begin to put in details and refine the outlines, I always use brushes at less than maximum opacity in order to use the transparency for shading.

STEP 3

Now that I have a nice basis for the head, I can start to paint the eyes, with a skin color a bit darker. I also use this color for dark areas of the face to work more on the depth.

I do portraits when I want to do a complete drawing on the iPhone, but I've found the iPhone a great digital sketchbook, great to begin a sketch or an idea when you're not at home and continue it later on your desktop!

STEP 4

I put in the first strokes of the hair. Again, I choose a color that is within the range of the original two colors to maintain a unified palette.

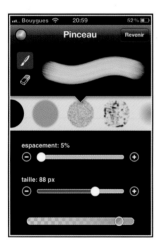

I love a traditional art exhibition, because it's a pleasure to be able to talk about your work with people who come to visit your exhibition, to meet people in real life, to share something special with them. But it's also amazing to see that, with one click, your work can be seen by the entire world with internet access. When I get feedback from someone who lives in Australia or Venezuela, I'm totally amazed.

STEP 5

I start shading the hair and the eyebrows. I love drawing eyebrows because they make up a large part of the facial expression.

STEP 6

I start adding details in different parts of the face, the eyes and the hair, and choose a glowing red to bring out the eyes from the face.

I choose the shading for the color of the hair to outline the eyes and soften the red. To play with the eyes and to create a link between the face and the background, I add some fuchsia lipstick.

STEP 7

To strengthen the depth of the piece and the neck's depth, I add purple variations to the background.

STEP 8

For finishing touches, I use a fine brush to put some motion into the hair with the same color as I've used for the shading.

STEP 9

I put more shading details on the lips to give them some gloss, and I also continue to outline the eyes with eyelashes.

STEP 10

In order to dress her up a little bit, I draw earrings using the same colors as the eyes, and demonstrate how one color and two tones, one light, one dark, can bring objects up from the canvas.

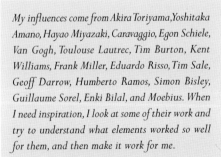

My influences come from Akira Toriyama, Yoshitaka Amano, Hayao Miyazaki, Caravaggio, Egon Schiele, Van Gogh, Toulouse Lautrec, Tim Burton, Kent Williams, Frank Miller, Eduardo Risso, Tim Sale, Geoff Darrow, Humberto Ramos, Simon Bisley, Guillaume Sorel, Enki Bilal, and Moebius. When I need inspiration, I look at some of their work and try to understand what elements worked so well for them, and then make it work for me.

I began my art career exhibiting traditional paintings and now I also do illustrations for children's books, comic books, and games.

Boys at Work

BY JOEY LIVINGSTON
Artist, Web Developer
Florida, USA

Joey Livingston starts with a story, then illustrates it in the app "Brushes". He takes us along for the full tour in his important discussion of light and creating the illusion of depth.

The iPhone and iPad have had a drastic effect on my growth as an artist. They have brought back the freedom that I had when I used a paper sketchbook, with many of the extra benefits that a digital art platform offers. For artists, the iPhone is essentially a graphics tablet in your pocket, something I wouldn't have dreamt possible more than a few years ago.

STEP 1

Painting on the iPhone and iPod Touch isn't so different from painting in any other digital or natural medium. The fundamentals still apply. We begin with a simple sketch to establish the overall composition. The line work here shows the sketch at a pretty advanced stage, which will provide an excellent roadmap for the piece.

JOEY LIVINGSTON
Painting Multiple Light Sources Creates the Illusion of Depth

STEP 2

We want to illuminate the room only slightly, with the sunlight coming in from the window, to give the impression that they had been working all night, into the wee hours of the morning. On a separate layer, we paint the garage as if no one was in it. Focus on the ambience of the morning sunlight pouring through the upstairs window and through the rails around the upper level. Gently work the shadows into the area below. Finish all the details of the objects hanging on the wall and on the shelves.

My most admired artists are offbeat comic book artists, like Cyril Pedrosa, Kazu Kibuishi, Jake Parker, and Rad Sechrist, just to name a few. The artists who have influenced me most are the ones who tell really interesting stories with their artwork, whether it be with just a single painting or a series of panels in a comic book. My very favorite artists have always inspired me to create entire worlds within the confines of a canvas.

The biggest advantage of painting on the iPhone or iPod Touch is the use of layers, which allows you to separate the background objects and the foreground objects into separate paintings that lie on top of each other. This is probably the thing that, most of all, separates digital painting from natural painting; with natural mediums, particularly the more opaque mediums like oil and acrylic, you really have to worry about painting all the background objects first and your foreground objects last, so that you don't end up having to paint around your foreground objects. With layers in digital painting, you can paint the backgrounds and foregrounds with complete disregard to the order you paint them. As long as you stay focused on how the color, lighting, and composition of each work together, things usually end up falling together nicely.

Boys at Work was a journey back into my childhood. I never built an aircraft, but I always fantasized about building stuff like that and going on incredible adventures with my friends. I have two kids now, and I watch them run around the house and the backyard, my son pretending he is a fireman or a monster, and my daughter pretending she is a princess or a teacher. It brings back those memories for me. One of the best parts of having kids is how it lets you relive your childhood through their eyes.

I'm a member of tons of groups on Flickr. If you had told me as a teenager that I would be able to publish my work in the blink of an eye, and hundreds or thousands of people would see it and even give me feedback, I don't know if I would've believed you. From my perspective, the computer and the internet are two of the greatest inventions of all time.

STEP 3

Once the garage is complete, we begin painting in the foreground colors on a new layer. We use the original sketch to lay over the top of the whole piece and provide extra definition to the forms of the boys and all the objects in the garage. The dim light provides an opportunity for some really interesting highlights created by the other light sources we created in the room, the fluorescent desk lamp and the welding sparks. Both of these sources produce a good bright blue light, which contrasts nicely with the deep oranges and yellows produced by the daylight. The sharp light that they provide contrasts nicely, not only in color but also in effect, to the morning light. You'll notice that the effect of the morning light is somewhat soft and subtle on the boys' heads and backs, while the light from the lamp and sparks has a very sharp, defining effect on the profile of their faces to finish off the piece.

Batgirl
Batgirl
Batgirl
BATGIRL
BATGIRL
Batgirl
Batgirl
Batgirl
Batgirl
BATGIRL

As a young girl I read a lot of super-hero comic books and watched kitchy TV shows like Batman. My work is influenced by pop culture icons of my youth and it's no wonder that these images have stuck with me and find their way into my work.

I created the BatGirl image using the "Inkpad" app. Since I have no experience with computer graphics and vector-based drawing I taught myself the app through trial and error and without any preconceived notions. I wanted to give the drawings a more hand-made look of paper cutouts or collages. I saved the image to my camera roll.

BatGirl

BY RITA FLORES
Artist
New Jersey, USA

One of my favorite iPad apps right now is "Inkpad". I like to use my "Inkpad" drawings as the jumping-off point of the paintings, adding elements such as words from "WordFoto" and textures using "Pic Grunger". I make several versions of the same picture and then use "SketchBook Pro" to create layers and erase unwanted areas.

I opened the image from the previous step in the app "Pic Grunger" to give an aged look and some character. I didn't worry that there was grunge in all areas of the image, since I knew it would be used selectively as a separate layer. I saved this to my camera roll.

RITA FLORES
Inspired Collage

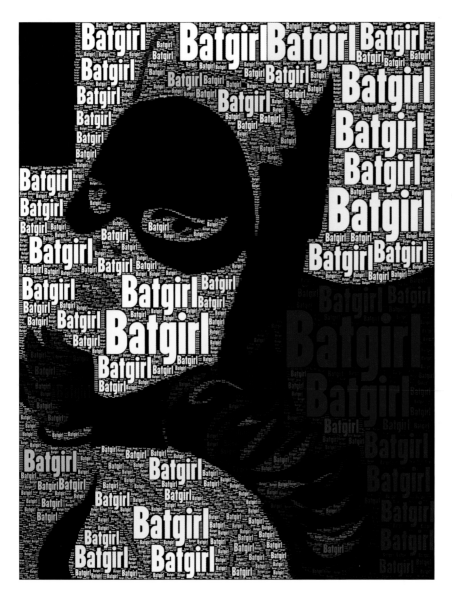

I opened my original "Inkpad" image in the app "WordFoto" and created two variations using two different fonts, saving both to my camera roll.

This app allows you to import a photo from your camera roll and then define the text that makes up every area of the image, with variations.

To finish the piece, I brought the four variations into "SketchBook Pro" as separate layers. The bottom layer is the original "Inkpad" drawing at 100 percent opacity. The next layer is the first "WordFoto" variation and I've erased 80 percent of it, revealing the bottom layer. Next comes the second "WordFoto" variation with different areas erased to reveal and highlight different words. The fourth layer is the "Pic Grunger" image at 100 percent, but with half of the image erased. The top layer is a duplicate of Layer 4 at 26 percent opacity and with different erasures.

In addition to working on my iPad, I still work with traditional media and take figure drawing classes, including Dr. Sketchy's anti-art school in NYC. I love to draw with pencils and am also working with acrylics.

I exhibit my mobile digital art on various groups on Flickr, Twitter, iCreated, Gallery, Etsy, and on my own blog, "Through the Lava Lamp".

In addition to my extensive online presence, during the past few years my iPad art has been included in real world exhibitions in the UK, Norway, California, Texas, Maine, New York, Wisconsin, New Jersey, and Washington, DC.

For the most part, I paint colorful "Expressionist" paintings of my traveling experiences. Art apps like "Brushes" actually invite me, through their easy interface and likable tools, to experiment and get outside any normal style. It's ironic that for a seemingly small work area, this new way of creating is refreshing and offers a new freedom for the artist.

I normally work in acrylic and oils on canvas and watercolors on paper, and to break the day up, I enjoy creating wood folk art. I'm also an avid movie-maker, using Apple's "iMovie" and "Final Cut Pro" to document the creation of my art and of lifestyle videos of travels.

PICTURE 1: THE ROUGH SKETCH

For this painting, created in the "Brushes" app, I wanted to create the feeling of a gentle summer day at the beach. A strong horizontal composition will help convey a lazy, easy feeling. So first I sketched the outline with a solid #1 brush at 1 px width using a light teal color at 100 percent transparency.

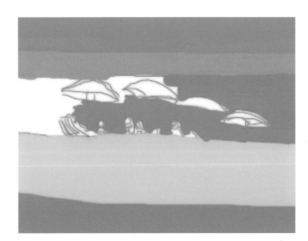

PICTURE 2: BACKGROUND COLORS

I used the slightly textured #2 brush with about a 40–50 width px diameter at 100 percent transparency from the color wheel to lay in the sky, ocean, and beach, being careful to totally cover the areas so no white shows through.

A Summer Day

BY MICHAEL P. IVES
Artist
Arizona, USA

This talented artist gives a detailed description of his methods in the app "Brushes" in the creation of his piece *A Summer Day.*

MICHAEL P. IVES
Painting an Atmospheric Seascape

PICTURE 3: SIZING

By pinching with my thumb and index finger to enlarge the image, I again use the #2 textured brush but reduce the diameter to 10–15 px at 100 percent transparency and begin laying in the brightly colored umbrellas and, by reducing to a 2–3 px width, some of their shadowing.

PICTURE 4: PERSPECTIVE

"Brushes" allows you to go in and out of full frame with a double-tap of your finger to see how it's coming along. It's a good idea to use this tool many times during the painting process. In this picture, I've gone back to full frame and can see that everything is clean and I'm ready to proceed to the next phase.

PICTURE 6: THE FINESSE OF TRANSPARENCIES

Now that the basic colors and composition are laid in, the painting begins to come to life. I use the #2 textured brush at varying sizes for the sky, ocean, and beach, with the transparency down to only 10–15 percent, and begin "finessing" each area with thin layers of pinks, teals, light yellows, all overlaying to create the impressionistic effect of movement of light.

I was raised in a small town in Ohio in the 1940s–1950s. I am a self-taught artist. I moved to Tucson, Arizona, when I was twenty years old and began drawing cartoons while studying architecture, taking many breaks to travel Europe and as many islands as I could. I joined the Peace Corps when I was thirty-five and taught architecture in West Africa. For the last twenty-five years I have been a self-employed professional artist, traveling and for many years dividing my time between Tucson, Arizona, and Hawaii, with my wife Jill.

As a young boy I was influenced by the art and movies of Walt Disney, all types of comic books, and trips to the Toledo Art Museum, where my father introduced me to art. My favorite artists are Van Gogh, Cézanne, Gauguin, Matisse, and Bonnard.

To be able to quickly create a painting outside of my formal studio offers me a different mindset; I don't have to worry about being the serious artist and creating something important for a specific reason or market. Funny, when I allow myself this frame of mind and just let it happen quickly with my finger-tip, some of my best work often comes out.

PICTURE 5: SMALLER AREAS

I use the #2 textured brush, reducing the size to 3–6 px at 100 percent transparency as I paint in the smaller figures and the light bouncing inside the umbrellas.

PICTURE 7: CELEBRATE

Isolated swatches of unexpected red and orange celebrate and divide the long horizontal format. Use the #2 textured brush, 5 px width and 100 percent transparency. To smooth out the strength of the red, I keep my finger down on the teal water next to it (which selects that color with the eyedropper tool), put the transparency down to about 20 percent and move it over the red until it's softened to my liking. This last step is repeated many times throughout the later stages of the painting to help give a softened overall effect as I finish detailing the people, chairs, and umbrellas.

Sometimes important things aren't realized until people reflect back after time. I went to Woodstock, and like everyone else only later realized the scale of what had happened. I've got a sneaky suspicion that we are experiencing much the same thing today as the mobile digital art world comes of age.

PICTURE 8: MISTS OF COLOR

I want to give the painting an ethereal feeling—atmosphere, if you will—so once again I choose the #2 brush with a 10 px diameter and keep the transparency level way down to 5–10 percent, just pulling the existing color of the umbrellas up and away. Slowly it evolves. If it's too much, I can back-track with the always forgiving "undo" arrow (a wonderful tool).

Voila! The painting is now ready to upload to my online "Brushes" gallery where I can make high resolution copies for prints, post onto my Flickr groups, and download a movie file of all the behind-the-scenes strokes it took to create the piece. I like to then take this "QuickTime" video into Apple's "iMovie" and create a custom video with accompanying title, music, and narration for a professional look suitable for the classes I teach or for speaking engagements.

PICTURE 9: SIGNATURE

To finish off the painting, I use the #1 finest brush at 1 px width and a complementary color, pinching the image all the way up to 1,600 magnification so I can easily write with my finger.

I have always loved art that tells a story, that speaks of the human condition. Using my painting A Summer Day as an example, there is the personal narrative of a day on the beach in Hawaii with a group of my friends. At the same time I pay homage to Monet, Renoir, and the Impressionists by creating a quiet, restful atmosphere of soft dreamy tones sprinkled with strong touches of color. All these artists' influences are recognizable in the piece and yet it is distinctly mine.

The Smallest Subject

BY KEVIN BARBA
Artist, Creative Director
Illinois, USA

Kevin Barba uses "Brushes" for creating fine detailed paintings of one of earth's tiniest subjects, earning him a reputation as a master in the world of mobile digital art.

I started out sketching on the iPhone using the "Brushes" app when the App Store opened. Over the past few years many other great apps have come out but I find myself constantly going back to "Brushes" for its simplicity and speed.

Mobile devices have almost completely changed my own personal creative process. Always having a camera on hand has helped gather much more reference for my files than in the past. I also enjoy being able to scribble out rough ideas for work or home projects and save them immediately without worrying about which napkin had which idea. I really like being able to email a concept sketch to a client when not at home.

STEP 1: ROUGH SKETCH

In the app "Brushes", I start with a white background and use a middle gray color to sketch in the basic frame. I keep the lines loose and sketchy so that everything is just suggested at this time. Then once that is done, I rough in a simple shadow and build it up slowly with a low opacity brush.

STEP 2: COLOR LAYER

Fill in the ant's body with a red brown color at a medium opacity. I use this method to build up shadows quickly. I start slowly mixing in yellows and a hint of white to give the body and legs some tone value and to help suggest a "wet" look.

A lot of the art that I enjoy is based on monsters and creatures in everyday situations. I like to look at objects around me, whether at work or home, and think of what their life would be if they came to life and had eyes, mouths, and arms. Some of these characters found their way to custom sculptures I did using either poly-clay or found objects. I enjoy sculpting and acrylic painting and usually find myself doodling out my next project before the first one is done.

STEP 3: SHADOWS AND DETAIL

Now, with the basic colors filled in, I zoom in to complete detail work with dark browns, reds, and light yellows. At this stage I use the coloring process to better define the edges and some of the finer details in the leg joints and body intersections.

STEP 4: HIGHLIGHTS AND ATMOSPHERE

For me this is the fun part. I'll add a few more shadow blocks to the body before starting on the highlights. I work with a 50 percent opacity white or a 75 percent opacity gray to lay out the main reflection areas of the ant's body. My references for these are part instinct and part looking at reflective surfaces. For this one, a stapler that was on my desk was used as a guide.

STEP 5: FINAL TOUCHES

For these, I go over areas of the ant with a large brush with white at 10 percent or lower to help push back part of the ant's legs. This technique works to give the figure depth and the illusion of transparency.

I have found a great number of friends and peers on photo-sharing networks who keep this new medium exciting. Almost every day I find someone out there online who does some amazing piece of iPhone or iPad art and helps push the bar higher for all of us. Hundreds of people worldwide recognize my love of ants and my artwork has gained attention because of my connection to sites like Flickr. Reading feedback and tracking each image's popularity makes it very exciting when people really like something you created from your heart.

The backlight illuminated screen and white background make it great for creating a lively atmosphere and help add depth for sketches such as this front-view ant.

A few examples in this book detail the use of a layers feature in the app "Brushes". This painting was created in June 2009, months before layers functionality was implemented in the app, and was painted the way one would paint traditionally, from back to front on a single layer.

I start by blocking in the man swallowing the city, first as a rough sketch and then, in the next panel, add the details such as teeth, eyes, and shadowing.

Dreams

BY MIKE MILLER

Artist, Web Designer
Colorado, USA

Painting on mobile devices requires traditional skills and a plan. Mike Miller displays a method to his madness.

Next the night sky, which starts as a purple glow, then in the second panel darker tones are added with a wide, semi-transparent brush. Continue here with some stars created with a white, 1 px brush. The hair was defined with the purple glow, then painted brown.

I've loved comic strips since I was young. Bill Watterson, Gary Larson, Charles Schulz, Frank Miller, Mike Mignola, and John Romita Jr are my biggest influences.

From there, I started working on the city from his mouth outward, zooming in on the image and working with small brushes. It was really fun to add in pieces of detail to each building and get lost in the painting for several hours, painting with the tiniest strokes. One of my favorite details is the streetlights and their opaque glowing bulbs, done with multiple-sized "taps" of a semi-transparent white brush.

I work exclusively with "Brushes". I've tried them all (support the developers!), but prefer the interface of "Brushes" and its ability to output files large enough to make prints up to 16 x 24 inches.

Midway through building the city, I worked the grassy cliff into the scene as a balancing foreground element, starting with big broad strokes of opaque color in the panel near right, with smaller strokes for the grass and the details in the cliff in the middle pane, working on down to tiny brush strokes adding a closed door on the path to the cliff wall and the twisted tree with its tiny leaves.

I complete the cliff by adding a robot, who makes his home behind the door. By zooming into this small section of the image, I can paint the robot with small opaque brushes except for the glow from his eyes, done with a wider, almost transparent yellow brush.

Finally, I add the last two buildings up front, pushing the foreground forward to the viewer, increasing the feeling of depth and completing the piece.

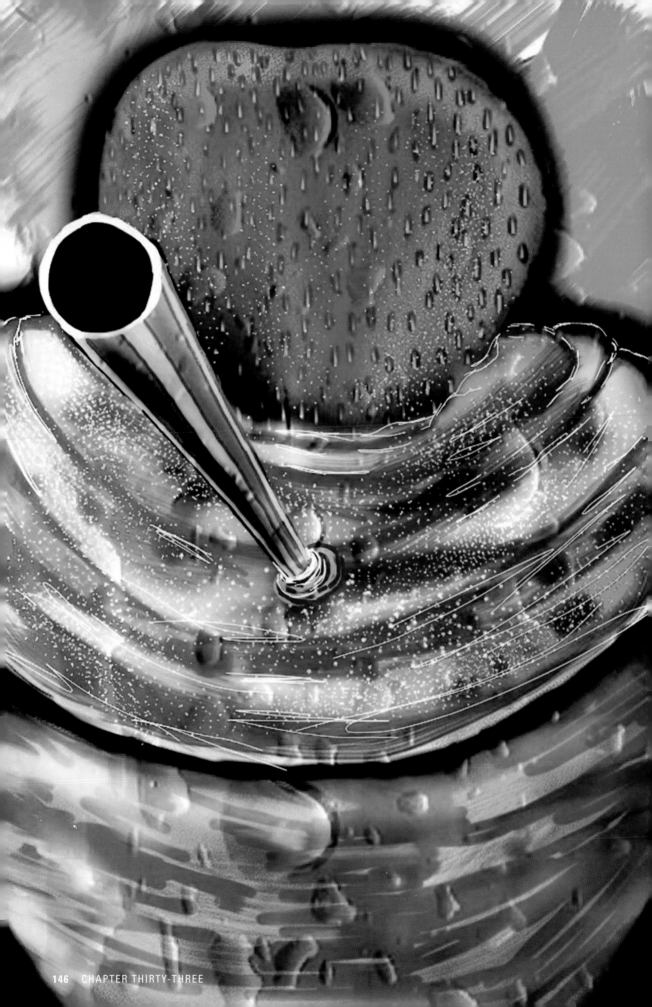

Strawberry Milkshake

BY WILLIAM KASS
Architect, Artist
São Paulo, Brazil

William Kass uses a layered approach in the app "SketchBook Mobile" to create a image that is both tactile and deep.

I'm from São Paulo, Brazil. I have lived here since childhood. I graduated in architecture from the University Belas Artes de São Paulo.

I do not have any procedure defined. First I think of something interesting to draw, more or less define the colors that I use and start drawing.

Within "SketchBook Mobile", I start by creating a few layers to set up the foreground and background of the drawing. I imagine the size and angle of the cup and start the first sketches.

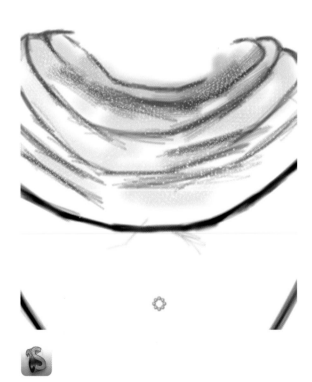

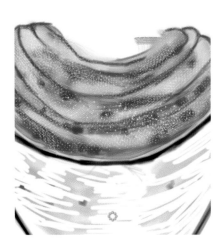

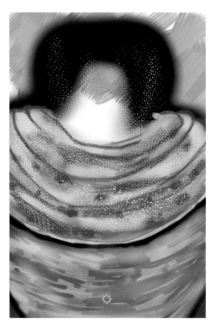

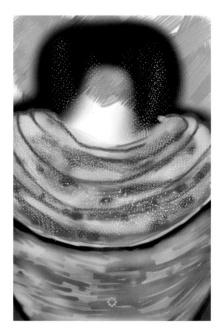

Then I start to draw and paint the milkshake.

Now I start to build up the background and prepare the place where I am going to place the strawberry. I use separate layers to paint on.

In the fourth stage of design, I paint the whole body of the strawberry, already in some detail. I used the airbrush and a pencil to create the strawberry.

You can view this and other works in my gallery on Flickr, where I also participate in various art groups on the iPhone. I graduated with a degree in architecture and have a strong artistic side. I think that architecture and art follow the same path. I love the work of Santiago Calatrava, Gaudí, Oscar Niemeyer, Picasso, Salvador Dalí, Jackson Pollock, among other architects and artists.

In the last stage I finish the straw and the final details of the strawberry. Now, the design is done in "Sketch-Book Mobile", but this is not yet the final artwork. After saving the image to the camera roll, I use two other apps to complete the design. The first is "Effect Touch" to improve contrast and lighting design and the second is "FX Photo Studio" to create the water drops effect. The effect of drops in "Photo Studio" serves very well for this job, but you can achieve this effect in "SketchBook" too, using different tools. That's it, the design is finished.

TIP The overlap of pure white highlights and pure black shadows helps create the feeling of depth, as does the straw's "vanishing point" into the milkshake.

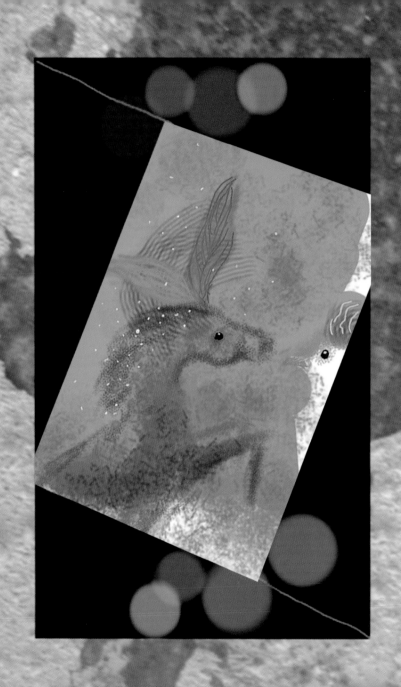

Tesseract

BY AMY NELP
Artist, Teacher
Colorado, USA

Amy Nelp develops her artwork in an unpredictable fashion, letting color and shape create a free association which leads to whimsical and spectacular results.

I grew up in Indiana and studied art under my father, who was a high-school art teacher. Upon retirement, he supported his family painting watercolors. I now live in Colorado and am constantly inspired by the beauty of the mountains that surround us.

Although I often have an idea in mind before starting to paint, this time I just felt like playing with color. In the "Brushes" app, I started with the first brush at a fairly large setting (20 px) and a fully opaque color, my favorite teal. Its shape suggests a field and its inverse shape suggests a bird to witness the progression of shapes and ideas.

AMY NELP
Soft, Lyrical Painting, Artfully Framed

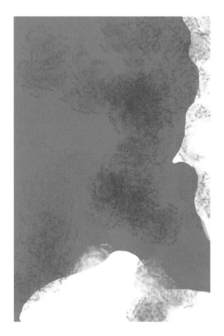 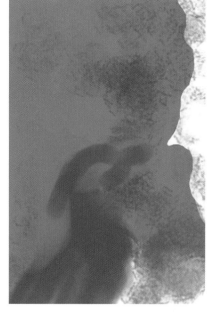 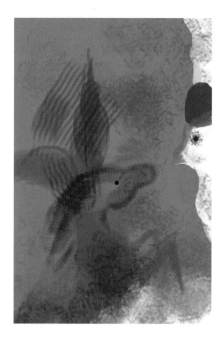

I introduce more colors, trying to build a textured area using the fourth brush, which has feeling of rough chalk. I set the transparency slider at 3/4 which gives me the texture that reveals the underlying color as well. Notice how much more organic it feels compared to the image at left.

I'm starting to see some other possibilities develop as I move to the fifth brush and softly add tans and browns. Some shapes, like the horse, become apparent and I develop it as the central figure of the piece.

For the top of the horse's head I paint with the tenth brush for the sponge-like effect, then back to using the fourth brush for more texture. I'm building depth and dimension by using various brush strokes on top of each other.

I continue to build textures with the fourth brush and then move to the airbrush #5 to soften selected areas.

At the time I began this painting, my third and fourth grade students were deeply involved in the book A Wrinkle in Time *by Madeleine L'Engle. It's a beautiful story, full of imagination, danger, suspense, fantastic situations, fantastic creatures, inspiration, and love. Gradually a horse-like character started to appear on my screen.*

As I painted him, I kept thinking about the book and its description of tessering (time travel and space travel combined) and thought my horse should just be coming back from his magical trip, not quite completely re-materialized yet. His strange friend on the right of the screen developed as more of a solid being who had been waiting for his friend in this unknown place. The plumes and the "magical" dots were included in the painting to show the elusiveness and wonder of the act of tessering. That's why I named this painting Tesseract.

I don't want harsh lines to define the horse's shape, so I use the last brush on a very small setting fully opaque. I then enhance the painting by using the two dotted brushes in different sizes, adding sparkle, glitter, and a decorative mane. This is then saved to the camera roll.

After finishing the original painting, I open the app "Frame Muse". This app has seventy frames to choose from plus the ability to rotate, resize, and reposition the image inside the frame. I open the image at left, pick a frame and place it as shown (right). Save the result to the camera roll. I open it once again in "Brushes", add some circles with the translucent #2 brush and finish with some thin white lines using a totally opaque #1 brush.

Nocturne

BY VALERIE BEEBY
Artist, Copywriter
London, United Kingdom

With an MA in English Language and Literature from Oxford and many years as a copywriter for British Airways and several large agencies in London and New York, this mobile artist has found a new love. Known on Flickr as 'The Purple Owl', she shows her experimental work in many groups featuring mobile digital art.

Valerie Beeby explores the use of texture to arrive at something organic and gritty. These two traits are not usually associated with iPhone and iPad art because the digital toolbox is perceived as technical, orderly and elegant. Now … maybe not.

STEP 1

The background to this piece is an out-of-focus close-up photo of my jeans taken with my iPhone. With sky above and earth below it conjures up storm clouds in the driving rain.

STEP 2

To create this painting, first I opened this background photo in the app 'Layers'. I added a new transparent layer and painted the waterfront buildings.

VALERIE BEEBY

Background and Texture: City and the Sea

STEP 3

Why work in 'Layers'? This app allows you to blend colours. Perfect for painting water. Opening a third layer, I laid down the sea colours in rough strips at 50 per cent transparency.

STEP 4

Using the blend tool, I smoothed out those crude lines in the water in the previous image. It was wonderful to see how the shimmer of the water appeared at the stroke of a finger. Blending done, the painting could now be exported to the camera roll.

STEP 5

From the gallery I opened the painting in 'Brushes'. The previous layers had been merged by the move, so I painted the moon, waterfront lights and reflections on a new 'Brushes' layer.

Inspiration? Modern art vs classical, and Drawing for the Artistically Undiscovered *by Quentin Blake and John Cassidy.*

STEP 6

The image was darkened by adding a new, transparent layer filled with a smoky grey. I positioned this layer below the one with the lights. Then I erased patches of the darkened layer to give a glow around the moon and its reflection. Notice how the original texture from Step 1 retains its presence in this version, which was then saved to the camera roll.

STEP 7

Finally, in the app "FX Photo Studio", I opened the image from Step 6 and added texture using the Ancient Canvas setting, followed by the filter Bump Map 1 to get a slight embossed look.

You can undo mistakes instantly, keep intermediate versions of your painting, mix oil and water and do all sorts of impossible things.

Literary study, various art courses in Italy and London, a life of travel, correspondent for a press agency and responsible for several communication projects, I put words and colors at the service of my imagination.

We start in the app "Brushes" with brush #1 to block in the horizon line, earth, and sky.

Use brush #5 to create a gradient of color in the sky painting with a range of tones between the yellow and red. Now we have our sunset.

Tuscany

BY MARCELLA DONAGEMMA
Artist, Correspondent
Rome, Italy

Painting on mobile devices takes on a decidedly 4th century feeling in the hands of this artist, who demonstrates her techniques with a few variations. What is unique here is that when the painting process ends, a new sensibility of image processing shapes the final artwork.

MARCELLA DONAGEMMA

Mobile Art Renaissance

To get some texture and detail in the foreground, use brushes #3 and #4 to add a few new tones of green. Our forest is starting to form.

Rough in the shape of the tower using brush #2 with a dark and light brown. The light brown helps to define the direction of the light source.

We use brush #4 to add some grain and texture to the tower using a similar brown tone.

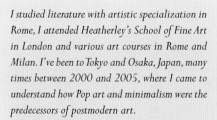

I studied literature with artistic specialization in Rome, I attended Heatherley's School of Fine Art in London and various art courses in Rome and Milan. I've been to Tokyo and Osaka, Japan, many times between 2000 and 2005, where I came to understand how Pop art and minimalism were the predecessors of postmodern art.

My traditional paintings are mixed media on canvas, acrylic, collage, and fabric. I lived for a while in Caracas, Venezuela, where the deafening colors of South America had a strong influence on my art and all my life. I have always tried to balance the relationship between color and feeling, reason and impulse: the search for harmony.

Life is a beating of wings and it's fabulous to trap a moment in a painting or a phrase.

Go back to brush #2 to glaze with a more golden color and roughly block in the windows. We have established the sunset in the sky, now we need to reflect that light in the tower.

We have the form, color, and composition desired, but seem to be missing the spirit of old that I'm searching for … We could leave it here, but I decide to take this magical place on a search for a soul.

Open the final painted image from the previous page in the app "Lo-Mob", and apply three different settings to the original, creating three different versions which are saved separately to the camera roll. The settings: "6 x 9 Instant Emulsion", "35mm Medium Format 2" and my favorite at right, "Saturated Vintage", which really expresses the feeling of an old, found painting. Perfect!

To create atmosphere, use brush #3 to soften the windows and create a more dream-like feel to the tower.

The final stage of painting this piece is using brushes 3–5 to create shadows and dimension to the foliage, the tower, and the tower windows. This is so important to show not just the sunset, but how the late light falls on the scene. Save this final image to the camera roll.

The Cottage

BY DAVID NAVAS
Painter, Illustrator, Animator
California, USA

What is unique here is this artist's methodology which helps define his vision. Using multiple references to color and composition, he refines his art to get to the core of his subject.

I'm an enthusiastic member of the photo-sharing network Flickr. This painting was an assignment for the Flickr group "Painting a Week on an Assigned Subject". Week 21 was Edward Hopper and my wife Judy and I were spending that weekend at a picturesque cottage in East Hampton, NY.

STEP 1

In the app "Brushes", I started by sketching out ideas and taking color notes. In this case, the color sketch made me realize that the important thing here was balancing the composition, the color, and the light.

STEP 2

I took a photograph of the scene for its accuracy of perspective. In the photo, the head was perfectly backlit and that provided a great visual idea that was used in the final piece.

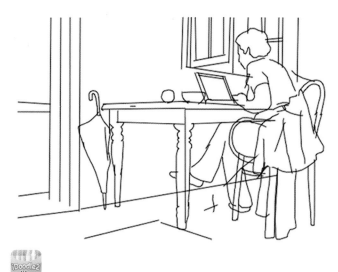

STEP 3

I opened the photo in the app in "iDoodle2" and traced the image by importing the photo as background and tracing it with the thin black pencil. Then I saved it to the camera roll.

TIP "iDoodle" is a vector trace program which creates a very uniform line and also allows you to fill precisely closed shapes with color.

STEP 4

I multiplied the traced drawing with a flat color in the app "Photo Canvas", as this app allows you to compose four layers using different modes (Multiply, Divide, Overlay, etc.). Then I saved it to the camera roll.

TIP I painted and blocked the darker areas first, as if I was painting with oil paint, and then gradually lightened up the colors and worked the highlights.

STEP 5

In "Brushes", I opened the traced image and put it on the top layer, putting the original color sketch on the bottom layer so I could use the color picker to select colors from the starting color notes. In this case, I can paint on the sketch layer since I want the lines to disappear.

STEP 6

Since this is a tribute piece to Hopper, I'm much more interested in limiting my palette and keeping my focus on composition and light. We finish a few details like the apple, the bowl, and Judy's arm painting in a very hi-zoom mode (400 to 800 percent) and picking colors from the surroundings. Save the image to the camera roll.

STEP 7

I open the image in the app "FX Photo Studio", and apply the Vintage Paper setting. This effect gives nice textures to some lighter parts of the painting and adds an overall warmth to the piece. We save the image to the camera roll.

STEP 8

I open it back up in the app "Brushes" for final retouching. This consists of erasing some of the texture so this effect is applied much more selectively, lightening up the color of the sky and, finally, changing the color of the bottom shirt hanging on the chair.

In *Trova*, created by Miguel Brambila in the app "Layers", the trovador pours his heart out in every stanza and breaks himself into little pieces, visually and figuratively, trying to express the beauty of poetry and music.

I started painting when I was sixteen in Mexico City. I had the opportunity to learn from great muralists and have been influenced by all the great Mexican muralists like David Alfaro Siqueiros, Jose Clemento Orozco, and Diego Rivera. Coming from painting walls that are 12 x 18 feet long to the 3.5 inch iPhone screen has been a challenge.

The World's Largest Mural

BY MIGUEL BRAMBILA
Artist, Social Services
Texas, USA

This artist details his process, technical and philosophical, to create and understand his piece *Trova*.

STEP 1
The first image is the outline of the composition drawn in the app "Layers" with a thin black brush at 100 percent opacity on a transparent first layer. This visual concept is the same if you are painting a mural on a wall or a painting on your mobile device.

STEP 2

I create a second layer filled with a solid brown background, which is then placed below the outline layer.

STEP 3

Now that I have the outline, I can start to fill in the final colors of the composition on the third layer.

TIP By placing the third layer I'm painting on under the outline layer and making it active, I can paint on it while viewing it through the top layer.

"Layers" was the app chosen for this painting because of its easy user interface to work with multiple layers, the option to email as a psd file, and the option to export a large file size through the "Layers" desktop interface. The app's thin brushes allowed me to create the lines that compose the broken trovador and his guitar.

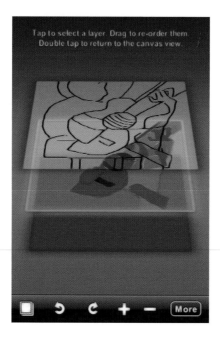

STEP 4

The remaining colors are painted in and, in some cases, slightly shadowed for the feeling of dimension. The guitar strings, hair, and signature are added as the final touches, using the finest brushes. Painting the guitar strings in straight lines was the biggest challenge of the piece.

Hoping to capture the beauty and trouble of a Trova singer or trovador, I used a somewhat Cubist image of a guitarist with his guitar. To play Trova or to be a trovador, a person should sing songs of his own composition, accompany himself on the guitar and deal poetically with the song. In a fast-paced world in which not even music has time to be heard and listeners prefer a catchy and repetitive tune with a total absence of feeling, thought, and musical genius, we have to open our ears to listen to this far from popular music genre: Trova.

Since I started to paint, first on paper, then on canvas, then murals and now on my iPhone and iPad, I have always tried to bring relevant ideas behind all the images to send a message in every painting. Sometimes Trova is also referred to as Cancion de Protesta (Song of Protest) which is very much related to what the majority of murals portrayed. I believe that art is a beautiful media to convey a message; if there is no message, there is no point in painting.

As I continue exploring this amazing new medium, my hopes are to send a message and to be able, someday, to make large, mural-sized prints of my work. With Flickr and other social networks, the idea of making large-scale (mural-sized) art might still be accomplished through the capacities of the internet, which might be, for muralists like me, the new, very large wall we can use to post ideas, and a worldwide audience for our murals even if they fit in the palm of your hand.

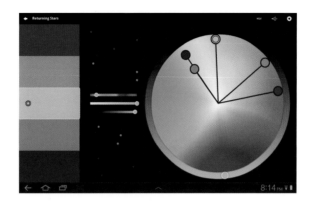

COLOURS

I began this painting by selecting five key colours to establish the mood of the portrait. Using 'Adobe Kuler' I exported the colours via the Creative Cloud to use later in the process.

Atmospheric iPad Portrait

BY KYLE LAMBERT
Artist
Manchester, UK

Kyle is a trained oil painter and illustrator from Manchester in the UK, who currently works as a freelance digital artist. He studied Fine Art Painting and Illustration with Animation at Manchester Metropolitan University and he specializes in creating striking images for storyboards, character designs and conceptual artwork.

Kyle creates his latest mobile art through a host of apps from Adobe. He shows his considerable Photoshop Touch 'chops', fine-tuning his portrait and showing us how it's done.

COMPOSITION

With the colours selected, I sketched a number of potential compositions using 'Adobe Ideas'. On a separate layer I then quickly mocked up how I was going to apply my chosen colour scheme.

NOTE   The key is to understand where the light is coming from and to add the necessary highlights in the eye. If you are new to painting portraits it may be worth gathering research or photographing a model to help get an understanding of how your portrait should be painted.

TONE

I imported my final composition sketch into 'Adobe Photoshop Touch' and created two layers: one white layer to mask the edge of the face and a second layer beneath it to paint the basic tonal values of the face using the paint tool. I then turned my focus to painting the detail of the eye using a smaller brush. The eyes are always a great challenge when painting a realistic portrait because they are such an important part of a person's identity.

OPACITY AND BLUR

Using a paint brush with low opacity I gradually built up the dramatic lighting of the portrait in greyscale. To soften the shading I occasionally used the blur tool. With the head painting complete, I then removed the white mask layer and proceeded to paint a background on a new layer beneath the head. I painted very loose shapes to suggest a city background and used the Gaussian blur effect to give the look of depth of field.

The viral nature of the internet is incredible. In 2009 my first iPad painting video, which I uploaded to YouTube, exploded and drew a lot of attention to my work across the world. It is such a great platform to get fast and varied feedback from fellow artists and people who enjoy your work. It has certainly changed my life and allowed me to meet and work with some amazing people. For Apple's announcement of the iPad 2, I appeared in a promotional video for the keynote presentation. Apple flew me to Rome and filmed a sequence of me creating an iPad painting of a lady in an Italian restaurant; see it at http://www.youtube.com/watch?v=RTygZhA7WFU.

COLOUR AND BLEND MODES

With the greyscale portrait complete, I then began introducing colour to the image. I created two coloured fill layers and used Blend modes to combine them with the painting: a yellow layer with the Multiply Blend mode to replace the light areas and a red layer with the Screen Blend mode to replace the dark areas.

GRADIENT COLOURS

Happy with the red and yellow colours, I then added green to the background to balance the image. To do this I did a Copy Merge of the whole painting and pasted it to a new layer. I then used the Multi Gradient Map filter to alter the colour range by adding the two green colours from my initial colour scheme.

EFFECTS AND DETAILS

I then used the Add Fade option to composite the new colours into the background only. I created snowflakes on a separate later and used the Directional Blur effect to give them movement.

I get inspiration from numerous sources. I am a big film and animation fanatic so much of my work is inspired by movies. The rest of my inspiration comes from the world around me. I think my love of film comes through in the way that I frame images and create atmosphere in my paintings. When I am working on an idea I am always trying to establish the mood of my idea through my lighting and colour choices. I try to do everything for a reason.

FINAL TOUCHES

To finish the painting off, I continued to experiment with the range of effects available in 'Photoshop Touch'. I used the Add Gradient tool to add a vignette and added the Grainy Night and Scratches effects to complete the image.

Cathie Morning

BY MIC REES
Artist, Graphic Designer
Lake Cathie, Australia

Artist Mic Rees paints in quick stabs of color. Using the eyedropper to sample color, and varied brushes to wash and detail, he shares his technique of watercolor on mobile devices.

I have tried some of the other apps but haven't found one that matches the ease of use and features of "Brushes". After painting in programs like "Photoshop" and "Painter" on the desktop, "Brushes" feels natural and you don't need to search through menus and palettes, you just paint.

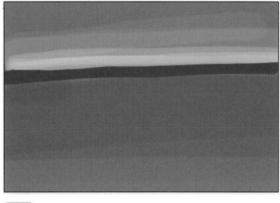

STEP 1

I approach the painting the same way I would a traditional painting. First, establish the overall color scheme and block it in to fill the canvas. Try to capture the feel of the subject quickly in its basic form to keep the painting fresh and active.

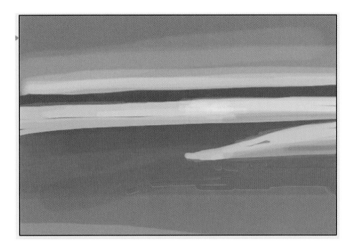

STEP 2

Next I block in the foreground using quick gestures and the basic rich colors of the subject. Sometimes I will take several swipes at getting the brush gestures just right (that's when the undo option is great in "Brushes"); it's like a electronic turps rag to wipe off the last brush stroke.

TIP The transparent option on the colors palettes and how it holds the transparency until you change it (handy if you are doing washes or building up a color gradually) is an incredible feature.

POGO Sketch Sometimes your finger gets a little close to the screen and blocks what you are painting. That's when I discovered the Pogo Sketch—great if you are accustomed to a Wacom Stylus or just like to back off the screen a bit ... you do get more control with the zoom using both fingers and some different results.

STEP 3

I start painting in some details, not a lot but just enough to give the feeling and suggestions of detail. The undo feature is great if brush strokes don't work out. Just back the painting up a few steps, and try again. Sometimes I duplicate the painting in progress and try a different direction.

STEP 4

Using the sample tool and brushes with transparent colors, I just grab and wash areas with color forward and back. (Use transparency as tints, as you would a wash traditionally, only with a undo!)

STEP 5

Still grabbing colors and using them as a light wash, I finish with the greens to add contrast and then some 1 px strokes to add a visual focus to the piece. Finally, my signature is added. As soon as a painting is finished it can be uploaded to Flickr or Twitter, or emailed to someone, so you have instant feedback, good or bad. The file can be imported using "Brushes Viewer" on the desktop as a high-resolution file. From that file I make 8 x 10 prints using ultra chrome pigment inks and archival paper in editions of twenty-five.

I was traditionally trained in painting and then graphic design, and the two fields merged when I started digital illustration for magazines in Australia. I discovered the Wacom tablet and started digital painting with a traditional approach about ten years ago and haven't looked back. Then the iPhone, and "Brushes" came along and meshed as a great little companion and alternative for my bigger work. The iPad makes the process even more enjoyable.

A handy sketchpad in my pocket I can use whenever I get inspired, day or night.

reesdigital.com

Katana Jack

BY XOAN BALTAR
Artist, Graphic Designer,
Illustrator
Ourense, Spain

Xoan Baltar is an mobile art
pioneer. While there are now
hundreds of artists using these
tools, Xoan was there when
there were but a few. Here he
shows his talent and inspires
others with his "Brushes"
tutorial.

This tutorial is actually a background image in the App,
"Katana Jack!" by Ivanovich Games. Katana Jack! is
a tribute to the classic arcade game Bomb Jack, with
a little nuance, all the graphics have been painted by
Xoan Baltar on the IPad, with the app Brushes. As we
move through the different levels of the game, you can
unlock videos that are actually movie files generated
by the app, allowing us to see the painting process
step by step. It is not surprising that the artist who was
one of the first mobile digital artists and an inspiration
to so many, is also the artist who take this artform to
the next level. The game feature 90 levels that take
place in 15 of Xoan's iPad painted environments and
contains 28 videos with "Brushes" video playback.

At first when we create a representational image, we
start with the predominant colors, which in this case,
to portray a cloudy day, are gray and pale blue.

Then we can devote time to illuminating the scene, following with a brush a little thinner than in the previous step, and now we need some perspective lines, following the point of origin. Apply more vivid colors; nature is full of colors, one need only observe them. It's incredibly interesting how many shades and colors can be found in a scene.

As in the first step, use broad strokes on canvas to create the lights in this scene. The feeling of light at night, important light, produced by street lamps, is very exciting.

TIP First, I created a green street lamp on a separate layer, then duplicated it many times, resizing it, repositioning it, changing the color to yellow and repeating on the lampposts.

Paint the light points but with a clear tone, as this will create that magic "aura" around the lights ... Also start defining the background of the scene; although it is in the background, the main focus is the end of the street. This is not always important, but in this picture the remarkable thing is the depth of field and the views that occur in large cities.

Finally, concentrate exclusively on the lights and reflections in this scene. I have chosen to depict the light trails left by cars, a very pretty effect created with a set of fantastic colors. Lampposts, previously drawn with a finer brush and a much lighter color, are painted at the center and give the effect of realism; the rest of them are lines for perspective. Would you call this style fast and inaccurate Expressionism? If indeed it is that, to give them a time context, these sketches are completed in five or ten minutes with quick and expressive strokes. This lends the scene much more character and realism. And the iPad allows this, as fingerpainting is fantastic and you don't have to wash your hands afterwards. Finally, I've framed this scene in a box, for a more elegant presentation on internet galleries. I'm passionate about drawing. Does it make my spirits soar, like flying? Yes, it does.

I live in northern Spain, in Galicia, and studied at the School of Art Anton Faílde of Ourense. I work in advertising as a freelance graphic designer and illustrator, and also create a newspaper comic strip.

I have enjoyed the arts since childhood, and have painted in all known techniques and experimented with many not so well known. Art itself is a constant experimentation.

I am influenced by all the masters of painting: da Vinci, Picasso, Michelangelo ... but I like art in general, and anyone who ventures to experiment and explore the world of creation.

2009
SEYDEL

Bird Brain

BY MATTHEW SEYDEL CONNORS
Illustrator, Retoucher, 3D artist
New Jersey, USA

Matt Connors demonstrates the building of an image with density, intensity, multiple apps, a touch of art history and a sense of humor.

MATTHEW SEYDEL CONNORS
No One Calls Me a Bird Brain + 3D, Abstract, and Background Elements

This image begins with a few quick strokes using the "Jackson Pollock" app. "JP" is a very liberating app to use because it goes against every instinct an artist might have regarding technical precision. Like the artist Jackson Pollock, you can control the color, quantity, and location of the paint, but not how it splatters on the canvas. My natural inclination is to develop a tight drawing, and "JP" is pure fluidity and right-brained goodness.

Open the result in the app "Fountain Pen", for adding more line and cutting back into the figure. I have worked with scratchboard and linoleum cuts in the past, and I wanted *Bird Brain* to have that tactile "cut-into" look and feel. Stroke recognition in "Fountain Pen" is quick, which suits my style of making many marks in quick succession. The app does not have a zoom feature, but this allows you to maintain a bird's eye view (pun intended) of the entire drawing rather than getting lost in the details. Again, when work is completed in this app, export the image to the camera roll.

The image is then imported to the app "TypeDrawing", which allows you to add text strings that follow your finger-painting strokes. You can add specific text thoughts in one of several font choices with color controls limited to variable transparency of black and white. Once these parameters are set, you are painting with a string of text, created as you move your finger across the iPhone screen. You can see in the image above how the text is scattered throughout the piece, adding an interesting new visual dimension.

The text that I used in the drawing is the repeated line, "No one calls me bird brain", used to heighten the self-consciousness of the figure.

The text from "TypeDrawing" is very precise and crisp; to break up the line quality, the image is reimported into "Fountain Pen" from the camera roll and additional white strokes are added.

Though the image is coming along nicely, it still looks a little cold and dry; my intent was to make it look like a discarded or aged drawing in the style of the Surrealist printmakers, like Salvador Dalí. The image is imported into the app "FX Photo Studio" where the Crumpled Paper filter is added.

Max Ernst, one of the Surrealists who has always has a special influence on my work, used birdheaded figures in many of his paintings.

Next, the image is opened in the app "Brushes", the premier iPhone painting app, which has several brushes that mimic the look and feel of natural media, with unlimited undos and an intuitive zoom tool and color picker. "Brushes" allows the user to edit brush transparency with two taps of a finger, accommodating smooth blended paintings. On the *Bird Brain* image, the roughest and most painterly of "Brushes"' tools is used to build more depth and shape to the character.

"Brushes" allows me to add the weight and detail that I want to the character, and reduce the crispness of the type and pen marks by using a smooth brush at low opacity.

This stage represents the level of detail I wanted to create in "Brushes", yet I felt the image needed warmth to make it more personal and compact.

I save the file and open it back in the app "FX Photo Studio" to apply the warm Vintage filter.

Above, the image with the Vintage filter applied has the necessary atmosphere, but the filter has flattened it visually. To increase the focus on the figure, the app "iRetouch" is used to selectively burn in highlights and apply more contrast, as well as clone stamp out some imperfections.

Once the dodge and burn is complete, the last step is the "Mill Colour" app, which allows for fast and intuitive RGB channel-based color correction. Completed image above.

Type and words have been used in images to great effect throughout the history of art.

SEYDEL

"Seydel on Soto", an AppSmash tribute walkthrough …

An AppSmash is any fingerpainting that uses more than three apps. To complete this image, I used seven different apps on my iPhone.

"Artisan" image exported to "Juxtaposer", then top robot head background erased.

Seydel on Soto

BY MATTHEW SEYDEL CONNORS
Illustrator, Retoucher, 3D Artist
New Jersey, USA

This artist creates elements using multiple apps to prepare for the final composite. Using 3D elements, abstract creations, and organic backgrounds, he constructs his final artwork in the app "SketchBook Mobile".

"SculptMaster 3D", shown above as the start of my painting, is a fantastic little app that allows you to sculpt a digital piece of clay in the color of your choice, then export the finished piece as a 3D model or as an image. The app allows you to rotate around your object, enable object symmetry, and smooth the surfaces that you sculpt. It's a lot like digital Play-Doh without the mess. I started with a fill of the maximum block size, then cut in eyeholes and a simple mouth to make a boxy generic robot head. Who doesn't love a robot, after all?

I had previously created a few color swirl images using the app "Artisan", and I used "Juxtaposer" to place the blocky head from "SculptMaster 3D" onto the "Artisan" image and erase the background, mapping the two into one composite image.

Often when I'm fishing for an idea or only moderately inspired for an idea for a whole painting, I'll work on components that I may be able to use in a later composition. This may seem counter-intuitive at first, but it can give you a lot of freedom to be creative, without having an "end result" in mind too early on in your ipainting process.

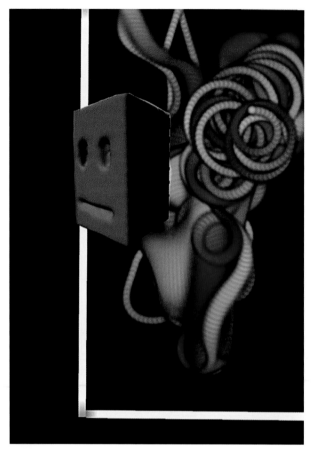

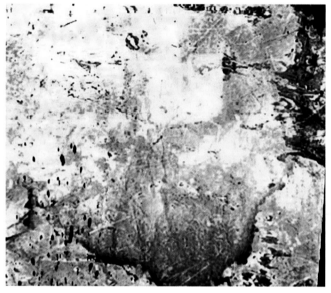

Though the image was still in an early stage, I felt a distinct tingly sensation down my spine that this looked reminiscent of the paintings of the amazingly imaginative Jeff Soto: http://www.jeffsoto.com/. I was inspired on the spot to make a tribute artwork to Jeff using my iPhone apps. I have the utmost respect for Jeff's work, so I needed to up the ante to make my homage.

The background texture needed to be bright and warm; I started with few quick strokes using "Inspire", then into "FX Photo Studio" to add a bit of texture with a filter … but it just wasn't "crunchy" enough. I imported the image into "Grungetastic HD" to add the sort of painterly grunge that I felt would make a fitting backdrop.

I pulled the composite image at right into "SketchBook Mobile" as a second layer, which gave me the freedom to erase the black areas and place another lighter image behind it to build more depth.

Throughout my artistic career my influences have been varied, from photography greats like Alfred Steiglitz to relatively obscure Renaissance artists like Ghirlandaio to contemporary street art and graphic design. In favor of one specific style, I choose to develop an array of different styles in traditional and digital media to apply to projects as needed.

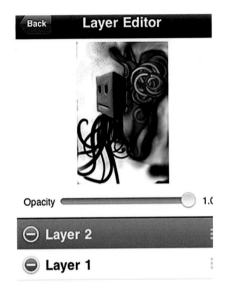

Back **Layer Editor**

Opacity ●————————○ 1.(

⊖ **Layer 2**

⊖ **Layer 1**

"SketchBook Mobile" has much of the muscle from its parent app, Autodesk's "SketchBook Pro". "SBM" has a quite intuitive interface and an array of customizable brushes that mimic natural media, whether pencil, dry brush, or airbrush. I used a large nozzle airbrush to overpaint some dark color to allow the background and foreground to sit more comfortably in the same image, then I made a new layer in the app to paint in more details.

At right, I've added several tentacled limbs to the bottom of the robot head, to give our automaton fellow a means to locomote. Once all of the major pieces were in place, I was free to experiment with the different "SBM" brushes.

The flexible nature of the layer structure of "SBM" meant that I could paint over the figure, then merge those details down while still maintaining the two layers for the main image and the background behind. This allowed me to relax and build up the detail in the image at my own pace. To keep the colors consistent, I sampled the colors from my original "Artisan" pic to make a custom palette in "SBM".

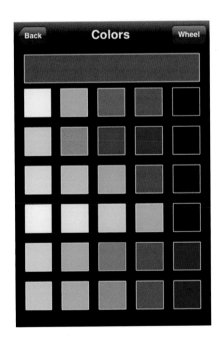

Back **Colors** Wheel

Chris Fayum Portrait

BY JOHN BAVARO
Artist, Professor
Pennsylvania, USA

Here we'll see how an artist might approach a subject with a very specific intent, and a method to match. We'll learn the steps to replicate art from another century.

The Fayum iPhone Portraits *are my homage to what are generally thought to be some of the longest surviving traditional paintings in history. The original portraits were done on wood using encaustic (wax) paints during the times of Imperial Roman Egypt (ca. 300 BCE to CE 300).*

In Stage 1, I try to approximate the light and pose from antiquity, and that tries to takes into account that there was no artificial light in CE 100. The portrait sitters for the original Egyptian Fayum portraits most likely posed during a certain time of day, in a window of time when the light was appropriately even and not too raking.

My model Chris posed near an open window for two quick iPhone snapshots. The warm, diffuse light hit his left side, while the cool daylight illuminated his right side, and that seemed like the perfect conditions for the painting.

I imported the photo into "Brushes", and painted with the brush spaced at about 30 percent, and at full opacity, then blocked in fields with the 25 brush by using the eyedropper to match local colors in the face. The result is a rough layer, with openings in it. I often save this layer as a separate painting to eventually merge its rough strokes back into the final piece.

Paint from general to specific, bringing the brush down in size, even to the #1 brush, as we put in details such as eyes, lips, and even mustache hairs. I find that at this point using the tool at 100 percent opacity is too heavy-handed, so we set the opacity at 40 percent or less so that we can layer semi-transparently.

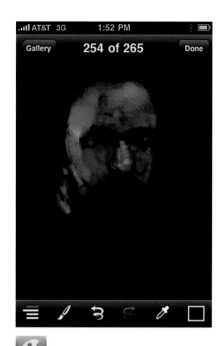

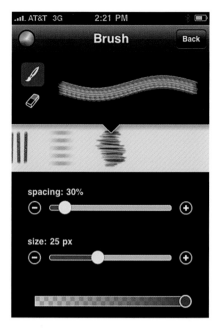

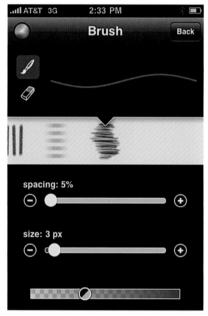

I'm a practicing artist, a college art professor, and an old-school oil painter, who was a bit awestruck when I saw what could be accomplished on such a tiny screen, and then exported to a high-resolution print.

In the original Egyptian Fayum portraits, the stakes for the artist to accurately "capture" this personality of a sitter were high, as the effigy had to serve as an accurate stand-in for the deceased for all of eternity. The better the likeness, the more likely that Osiris, the god of the underworld, might be inclined to shepherd their souls correctly into the afterlife. The head and shoulder-sized olive-wood painted piece was placed over the top of the actual face of the person's mummy, with the bandages wrapped around so that the face stayed exposed, so he or she could be recognized by the deities.

Original Photo.

Next step, we import a photo of a dilapidated piece of painted wood into "Brushes" on its own layer. The cracks and fissures prove perfect for my process, so we create a empty layer, place it below the photo layer and make it active to paint on. By reducing the opacity of the top photo layer, we "onion-skin" a replica, crack by crack, texture by texture, into a copy and then discard the original photo layer. Using the eraser tool, we begin to soften up the edges of the board to indicate ancient wear and tear.

Finally it was time to merge the two paintings, but first I had to place the cracks on top of Chris's face in a way that made him appear to recede. To do this, I erased "blindly" on his face layer, while it was submerged a layer down. I erased away little "rivulets" with the #1 brush to cause "spider cracks" on his face. I then brought this layer to the front, did some touch-up and clean-up, and then "weathered" the edges of the board more with the eraser tool. To capture a likeness is the first challenge of any portraitist and one that I've pursued my whole artistic life, but I find the second challenge

My mobile art is unapologetically photo-derived, but I see it as my burden as an artist to remove it far enough from its original source that it takes on a unique life of its own. Using the "Brushes" app, I'm able to build and merge layers of surfaces until I create an illusion of a "weathered" piece.

I hope that I not only am able to make good paintings, but can also provide some hidden commentary on this modern ephemeral medium by interpreting a most ancient technique with a most modern one.

I love the act of taking something so current and being able to manifest the "feeling" of these inspirational works in such an immediate way, to make art more than mere "pictures," or even mere "portraits". I love to see my friends portrayed as ancient Egyptians and to imagine them in those roles, while taking my own stab at eternity.

of making illusionistic, *tromp l'oeil* spaces to be the real envelope I try to push with my mobile art, especially for a piece like this, done on the small surface of my iPhone.

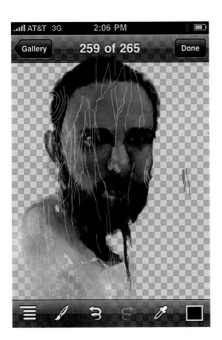

Infinite Zoom, Then Paint the Details

BY RUSS CROOP
Artist, Photographer
Colorado, USA

Versatile artist Russ Croop reveals his method of painting the finest elements in this early iPhone art masterpiece and the meaning of the words "perseverance" and "attention to detail".

My Living Room was a bit of an experiment to test the limits of the app "NetSketch". Since it is vector based, it allows for infinite zoom in and out and a seemingly unlimited canvas size. After having produced several very large sketches, I decided to see just how big I could go.

I spent seven evenings, as I sat watching TV, sketching my living room to complete this piece. When I started labeling the books on the bookcase, I knew it was going to be very detailed. As you can see from the finished piece at left, there was only one way to approach this image and that was a small chunk at a time. Below you can see sections of the piece, just so you get a sense of scale and the level of detail in things like book titles and guitar strings.

Drawing is achieved by using a finger or thumb as your brush. To create shading, you must go to the color picker and find a similar but darker or lighter shade of the same color.

The zoom feature is the key to this piece. Use your thumb and finger in the pinch motion to zoom in or out infinitely. Here we see the zoomed-in view of the lamp to the left of the TV. Without this extreme range of zooming you could never add the tiny details like the texture in the glass or the elephants.

TIP The middle icon at the bottom of the screen shows four arrows. Tap once and the image zooms out. Tap again and it will return to the close-up. This is very handy when doing large sketches since it's easy to lose your place inside the image.

Notice the circles on the speaker below the digital clock, and the yellow bulbs on the string of lights. By tapping once on the screen, you can create a perfect circle. The size of the circle can be changed by using the brush size slider and/or by zooming the sketch in or out. By zooming out, the relative size of the circle gets larger and, conversely, by zooming in, the relative size of the circle gets smaller.

This piece is composed with many straight and parallel objects like the books and shelves. You can make a perfectly straight line by placing your thumb on the screen where you want the line to begin and then tapping twice with your finger on where you want it to end. It takes some practice but it's easy to hit the undo arrow (fourth icon from left) and try again until you get the hang of it.

When I went to export the drawing it wouldn't complete the export and repeatedly crashed my iPhone. I finally emailed "NetSketch" app developer Ben Gotow and asked him if he had heard about the guy who built a boat in his basement and then couldn't get it out. I'd done the same thing with this image. Ben had me send him the entire iPhone back-up folder so that he could extract the file and send me the full-sized eps file. The final eps file weighs in at 85.597 x 70.931 inches at 72 ppi, and was printed as an 60 x 50 inch archival Giclee on canvas.

Simplify, Edit, Refine

BY RUSS CROOP
Artist, Photographer
Colorado, USA

Photographer Russ Croc illustrates his iPhor photography through h words and images, finding th some very basic photograph principles apply perfectly this new medium.

Russ Croop

Quite often, beginner photographers think that if they only had a better camera, a longer lens or some other piece of cool equipment, their photos would be fantastic. My reply is always this: If you hand an expensive camera to a beginner, it doesn't necessarily mean that s/he will take great photos. If you hand a simple, featureless camera to a great photographer, chances are those images will be impressive. It isn't the camera that makes a good photograph, it's the person controlling it.

In order to make really good images, the iPhone photographer must go back to the basics. Get close. Simplify. Determine the center of interest but avoid putting it in the center of the frame.

Use the Rule of Thirds. Look for interesting shapes, lines, colors, textures, and angles. Avoid contrasty situations. Hold the camera steady. Strive to "create" an interesting image—don't just "take" a picture.

The iPhone's camera has come a long way since the first 2 megapixel offering. Current models feature greatly increased resolution, better low-light performance, improved optics, faster processing, sophisticated focusing including facial recognition, a high dynamic range (HDR) mode, zoom, flash, video, and much more. These features rival and even surpass many stand-alone point-and-shoot cameras, making it a serious photographic tool.

Because I always carry my iPhone with me, I am ready to capture great images whenever they present themselves. I am less apt to feel the need to carry my DSLR with me and I find myself making images that wouldn't occur to me when shooting with the larger camera.

Perhaps the most unique thing about iPhone photography is that there are so many iPhone apps that allow you to edit, enhance, refine, manipulate, rework, slice and dice, re-imagine, and share your photos, The creative possibilities are limitless and profoundly inspirational.

Wonder started out with a simple iPhone photograph imported into "Photo Canvas", where the stars, bubbles. swirls of light, and the YES stamp were added to create this simple collage.

Fragile is a compilation of three photographs combined in the app "Juxtaposer". The rose photo was used as the background, and the two mannequin images were cut from their original photos using the eraser tool and positioned over the rose. The FRAGILE stamp was added using the app "Photo Canvas".

I photographed these shiny, nested bowls to create this self-portrait. I corrected the exposure and increased the saturation in the app "Photogene".

Section 2

Photography, Collage and Photomontage

...Photography as Art" debate is as old as photography. Early photographers sought to replicate the esthetic of painting with this new medium. Others pursued photography as a way to simply document the world around them. Since then, thousands of artists have created millions of photographs with artful intent. One thing cannot be denied … the evolution of modern art since the birth of photography has been profoundly affected. Over a hundred years later, we have witnessed a myriad of technical photographic innovations, each one a new tool in the toolbox and another means of expression to be harnessed in the hands of the right photographers. Photography as art is a debate that has been over for some time now, yet every leap in technology somehow still stirs up the question, "Is it art?" The act of taking a photograph, something that for the entire history of this medium required even the most basic camera, now is accomplished with the ubiquitous cellphone, and it is the camera.

But it is much more than that. It is actually many kinds of cameras, many kinds of lenses, many kinds of darkroom effects, and a digital photographic workstation in your pocket. For those old enough to have shot, developed, and printed their own photos in a darkroom, even those who became proficient "Photoshop" users, the leap to an iPhone and iPad for image editing can only be described as liberating and exhilarating. What we'll do in this section is look at a group of photographers who are using their iPhones to capture photographs and, through the use of specific apps, enhance their vision. This section also includes artists creating collage, photomontage, or "iPhone/iPad mash-ups", art created using multiple apps.

Early precedents to collage as art occurred from the invention of paper until the calligraphers of 10th century Japan, and again in the religious imagery of 13th century medieval Europe. It was Picasso and Georges Braque, at the heart of the Cubist movement

in the early 20th century, who invented the term *collage* (from the French word for glue) to describe this modern art method. Today, in retrospect, we can view their collages as the beginnings of modernism in art as the plane of the canvas is broken. The incongruous ideas contained in collage and photomontage were also the predecessor to Conceptual art as artists have this peculiar habit of breaking the rules, and exploring and expanding the boundaries once they are broken.

Then, after WWI, the Berlin Dadaists needed a word to describe their use of photography, the ultimate "readymade" element, included in their art. They chose *photomontage* because it expressed the mass produced, anti-art message they wanted to deliver. New technology would replace the elitist systems in place. They viewed themselves as art engineers assembling their art from mechanical reproductions (photographs, newspapers) being produced by the new world of mass communication. The roll call of modern artists who have used photomontage or collage as part of their body of work is long and impressive: in addition to Picasso and Georges Braque, we can include Matisse, Hannah Höch, Juan Gris, Man Ray, Kurt Schwitters, Max Ernst, Robert Rauschenberg, Tom Wesselmann, David Hockney, and the Starn Twins.

On the iPhone and iPad, the concepts of collage and photomontage are extended to include the infinite possibilities of the web. Do you need a texture, an element, a tiny scrap from the mountain of visual data pumped into the web every single second? The only thing that matters now is your idea, as any written or visual element created in the history of humankind is available, delivered directly to your mobile device. Copyright laws are to be taken seriously and the copyright of others must be dealt with respectfully, but the Supreme Court has already ruled in favor of artists' limited usage of copywritten material in their collages. The "Do Unto Others" rule is a good one to follow here.

The camera and the wide range of apps are there, all the time. If I'm moved to take a photograph and apply an app to enhance my vision, or alter the emotional content, I can. The process itself inspires me to create. I now approach the subject in a way that I wouldn't have originally thought of. Therein lies the power of the iPhone.

I opened my photograph of the George Washington Bridge in the app "CameraKit" applying B + W with LV.1 soft focus and +1 push processing. The result was saved and then opened in the app "ArtCamera" where the Burnt Paper effect was applied to complete this evocative final image.

Opened the "Dumpster" photo in the app "CinemaFX" and applied Charmed Glow on a low setting. The image was saved and then opened in the app "TiltShift Generator", where we use a medium circle of blur to retain focus in the center, increase the color saturation, and increase the contrast to finish the image.

Art, Life, iPhone

BY WILLIE COLE
Painter, Photographer, Art
Director
Connecticut, USA

Willie Cole, born into a world of art, now armed with a device to match his vision, details his iPhone art techniques.

WILLIE COLE
Art, Life, iPhone

Cinema Lights was opened in the app "CameraBag" and the 1974 effect was applied for its square format and its effect of muted color and increased contrast more reminiscent of the 1940s.

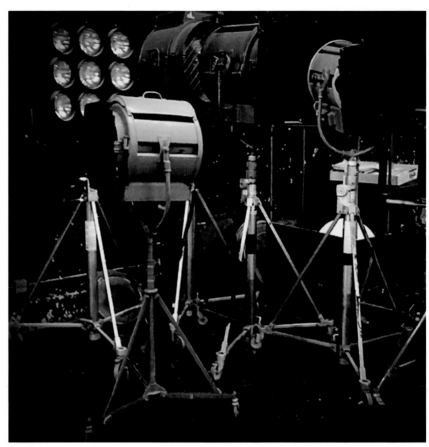

My earliest and fondest memories of being influenced by art are due solely to the fact that my father taught Art History and Studio Painting for 48 years at a private high school in CT. He was constantly talking about the power of variety and unity. I was exposed at a very early age to a diversity of art periods and styles but responded most to Abstraction.

I've been influenced by Franz Kline's black and whites, Barnett Newman's very large fields of color, Frank Stella's use of color and geometry, and Robert Rauschenberg's amazing understanding and sense of design. This period has left an indelible mark of simplicity, color, and most importantly design in our understanding of art. I am, and forever will be, trying to find the comfort in my own work that I get so intensely from theirs.

I opened the image in "CameraBag" and applied the Lolo effect to add the frame, pump up the ambient blue light and add more yellow to the sidewalk.

I opened the photo in the app "CameraBag" and applied Lolo, giving it that square format and pumping up the colors. Then I opened the result in the app "Mill Colour", to finetune the color.

I opened the image in "CameraKit", and applied yellow in the cross-processing to effect the saturation of the yellow lines on the tarmac.

Shooting this photo, I was initially intrigued by the graphic nature of the painted lines on the tarmac. As I pressed the shutter, and saw the bird fly by, I prayed that somehow the bird had been captured in that magical moment. Imagine the feeling when I opened the image from the camera roll and saw just how perfect that bird was.

The Golden Ratio—I only used two apps on this image, standbys since the early days: "ToyCamera" and "Lo-Fi". I would shoot the same picture over and over using "ToyCamera" set to Random, and saving my favorite results to the camera roll. You never know exactly what you are going to get with "ToyCamera", and the app "Lo-Fi" also reacts differently to the gradations, saturation, and textures of any given image. I loved playing with the two apps in tandem and creating combinations that work like subliminal narratives. Sometimes, my diptychs are created as graphic visuals only, but if the viewer sees some hidden truth, some magical message, so much the better.

Narrative iPhoneography

BY KNOX BRONSON
Composer, iPhoneographer,
Curator
California, USA

Immersed in the iPhoneography movement, curating the web portal "Pixels—The Art of the iPhone", Knox Bronson is one of the mobile art movement's strongest evangelists. Now he shares his own intense, highly saturated, bold and graphic work, plus a chunk of his esthetic.

Knox is a purist, stating unequivocally that the medium is defined by the iPhone itself: no off-device image-capturing or editing allowed.

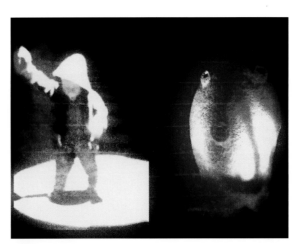

Spirit Guide—The little boy was shot in the SFMOMA under a tracking spot in the foyer. The creature is a piece of statuary in a nearby alley. I played with the color of both of these using the app "Photo fx", then added a fair amount of grain. I pulled them into "Lo-Fi" but they seemed ununified. I shot a picture of my rice paper shade in the living room and layered it in using "DXP". That seemed to tie both elements together, creating an image that's powerful and mysterious. The brain of the viewer can't help but create an association between two images combined into a diptych, but the real power of the piece lies with the artist's choices for those individual images.

Autoerotic—I took a number of shots of this little car in San Francisco's mission district one afternoon, thinking I would do the usual vintage-y grungy old car treatment. Using "Photo fx", I adjusted tints, contrast, cropping, and then I started noticing the design details and thought I might make a triptych … I assembled the images in the app "Diptic", looking for the right combination. I felt the image needed a little something, so I added grain using "Photo fx". The result is an abstraction, but with elements that feel tactile and somehow familiar.

Sun of Man—We needed an image for the flyer for the first Giorgi Gallery show in early 2010. I went to the hat store, got the bowler, and took pictures of myself, holding the mirror in one hand, my iPhone in the other.

The original shot required forty attempts, all using "ToyCamera" set to Random.

The original was cropped and desaturated for use as a poster and flyer.

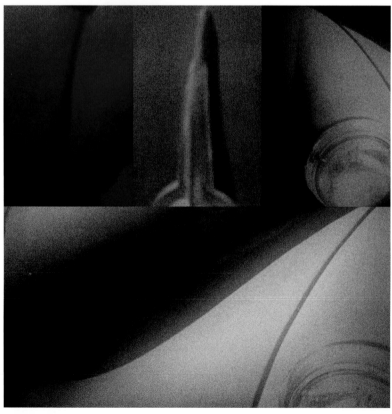

I used "Filterstorm" to adjust the color, toning down the reds and oranges, and brought it into "Photo fx" for a slight vignetting.

This piece is a homage to Magritte's iconic *Son of Man*, part of the joke being the Apple logo on the iPhone.

Bebe Gun—My friend Kelly's chihuahua, Bebe, is extremely photogenic: I've used her in several works, and in this frame her arms are folded back neatly and her look is right into the lens. The pattern in the left frame is the wallpaper in the rest room of my favorite Mexican restaurant. I got the idea for adding a gun, but I don't own one so I googled "handgun" and shot it off my computer screen, which added that great moiré pattern.

I layered the gun and the wallpaper together in the app "DXP", then brought both images into "Lo-Fi" to create the diptych. I find the juxtaposition of the two images quite humorous, although others have expressed various emotions such as horror or profound sadness. This is the beauty of combining incongruous images, where the net result in the mind of the viewer is always in doubt.

The Bottle—This was shot one sunny afternoon on Telegraph Avenue around the corner from where I live. Using "PhotoForge", I cleaned up a huge amount of litter and spots on the sidewalk, a painstaking process.

There were some other distracting elements behind the bus kiosk, including a poster where the red rectangle now is, and I cleaned them up as well. I hand-painted the red solid using "Effect Touch". I brought the picture into "TiltShift Generator" and made the bottle the focal point, lightly blurring the rest of the image. I then brought the picture into "Effect Touch" to further sharpen and highlight the bottle, which makes this image so poignant.

Sex Bomb III—The bottom image is a blue mannequin who lives in my kitchen. I call her Blue. I inverted the image and layered in the moiré pattern I captured shooting the computer screen with my iPhone. The mushroom cloud was shot off the television, and I brought both into "Lo-Fi" to exaggerate saturation and gradations of color. In "DXP", I layered different versions of the same image together and

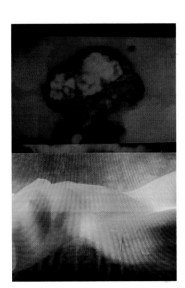

applied different layer effects until I found something I loved. I composited the final diptych in "Lo-Fi". Hot and cold, life and death; I wanted to create something bold and implicitly sexual, combined with the suggestion of utter annihilation.

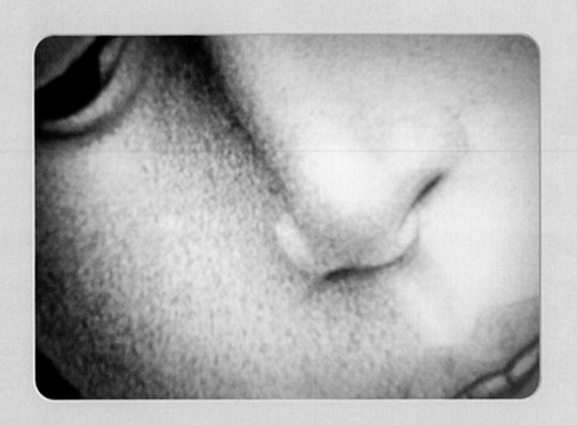

Figurative Photography

BY ANDREA MDOS
Artist, Photographer
Barcelona, Spain

The human figure has been compelling subject matter for artists since the beginning of time. Fast forward to the 21st century, where Andrea Mdos teaches us her approach to the subject using multiple apps to create her figurative art.

WINDOW

This was taken and edited within the app "Best Camera", using the Joya filter to increase contrast and color, and finally in the app "Lo-Mob", using the frame Slide 2 Warmer.

MOMENTOS

The image is processed in the app "PhotoForge", to convert the image to black and white, then opened in the app "FotoMuse", where we add a splatter layer giving the piece a hand-done feel. Finally we use the app "Cartoonize" to give the image a blur and remove it one step further from photographic reality.

MAKEUP

Photo was opened in the app "Toon-PAINT" to give it a comic book look and saved to the camera roll. Open that image in "addLib" to give it a graphic layout and then save it. We frame and crop the piece in the app "ShakeItPhoto".

THE FAREWELL

The photo was processed in the app "PictureShow" using the Multi Exposures filter to create the double exposure, then I cropped and framed the piece with "ShakeItPhoto".

SPANISH OLÉ

Open the picture in "ToonPAINT" to create a black-and-white image and delete the red from the original. Save the image and open it in "PictureShow" and use the Multi Exposures setting to create the altered composition. Save and open in the app "LunaPic" and use the Color Pencil Sketch filter to rough up the look of the piece. Open the image in "Lo-Mob" using the frame AE TTV DeSatured. Save and open in the app "CinemaFX" and use the Poster and Charmed Glow filter to reduce the color range and add blooming highlights.

SHADOWS

This image was shot with the app "ScratchCam FX" for the rough, organic feel and then altered in the app "Cool fx" where we use the filters Black and White, Hi-con 1, and Flashback to complete the piece and its dreamlike feeling.

4MEN

This image was altered with the app "FaceGoo" to soften the photographic lines of the figure of the man. Then I opened the image into the app "Lo-Mob", using the 6x6 TTV Green Virage filter to change the color balance, and finalized the piece in the app "Picture-Show" using the Quad filter to create this mysterious asymmetrical graphic.

iPhone Hipsta City

BY BETSY NAGLER

Writer, Film-maker, Photographer
New York, USA

Part control, part kismet, Betsy Nagler's images beautifully capture the graphic visual spirit that is the city.

The app "Hipstamatic" provides different effects that you can choose from before you take the picture, based on a variety of lenses, films, and colored flashes. These are essentially sets of digital effects that alter the brightness, contrast, colors, and border of the image to give it a particular look. Once you get familiar with the settings, you can get a sense of how the image will turn out, but there's always an element of surprise. You never know exactly what the package of effects, with the particular combination of lens, flash, and film you've chosen, will do to your shot. It keeps me on my toes and reminds me of how much fun it is to experiment and play in my photography.

TWILIGHT

Midtown office building, Manhattan. "Hipstamatic" app. Lens: John S. Film: Ina's 69.

This is an example of what's so great about iPhone photography: the camera is always in your pocket. This photo was taken while at work on a television shoot in an office building, with a view too incredible to ignore. The result, making use of the saturated colors and reflections, is a dream-like landscape which seems to exist in multiple dimensions. The rough edge added by "Hipstamatic" adds to the deconstructed feeling of the image.

REFLECTION 2

Midtown office building, Manhattan. "Hipstamatic" app. Lens: John S. Film: Ina's 69.

Here, the John S lens really made the colors at sunset pop. The combination of reflection and reality—including using the interior ceiling as a frame around the cylindrical building outside—created an interesting composition.

SUBWAY TRACKS AT NEWKIRK STATION

Brooklyn. "Hipstamatic" app. Lens: Jimmy. Film: Ina's 69.

Having the camera as a constant companion on the road changes the way I perceive the world; I'm always finding compositions, colors, and juxtapositions that I wouldn't see otherwise. This image was taken on the subway platform that I stand on practically every day, but having the iPhone made me see the peeling paint as a graphic element. I used the Jimmy lens because it highlights yellows and greens, which was just right for the color palette.

SNOW DAY

Prospect Park Tennis Courts, Brooklyn. "Hipstamatic" app. Lens: John S; Film: Float.

This was taken on the day of the third big snowstorm of 2010. For this photo, we chose the John S lens, which is great for the way it saturates colors and increases contrast in often unexpected ways. We also use the Float film setting, because it gives the photo a misty, washed-out cast, to enhance the timeless look of the scenery.

Being able to publish the photos to Facebook directly from the app, with all of the lens, film, and flash info, is great. That way you can check out what your Hipsta friends are doing and what other effects you might want to try out.

SHOOT AT THE HELIPORT

Downtown, Manhattan. "Hipstamatic" app. Lens: John S. Film: Blanko.

One great thing about working in film production is that we work at all sorts of interesting locations. Here's another example of being on a job at the right time of day and having the iPhone with me. With the taxis and police cars working as props, this image was very much about my New York: a city with a film set in the foreground. The John S lens was used to increase color saturation and contrast.

Deconstructing Photography on the iPhone

BY THOMAS A. MARINO
Artist, Photographer
Massachusetts, USA

While his focus is currently on altered iPhone photography, Thomas Marino's background is that of conceptual artist, whose work includes installation art, altered hand-made objects, photographs, and paintings.

While most photographers seek focus and clarity, this artist finds his niche using various apps to "take down" his photographs, seeking a new truth.

The photo *Still-life* (opposite) was shot with the app "Camera Genius" then opened in the app "Lo-Mob", where it was given a blue tone. In the app "FotoMuse" the image was framed in a distressed fashion, to further deconstruct the original image.

The woman's profile was shot with the iPhone app "Camera Genius". That image is opened in the app "HiCon Pro" to increase the contrast, then opened in the app "ezimba" to soften the image in a painterly way. Finally, the image is opened in the app "Foto-Muse" to frame the image.

For the *New York Times*, image, multiple photos of the newspaper were shot using the app "Camera Genius" and opened in the app "Montage", creating the composition at right. Then the image was altered using the app " Lo-Mob", giving it a distressed look. Finally, the image is opened in the app "Photo Finish" to give the piece a frame reminiscent of spilled ink.

This image was shot with the app "Camera Genius" and desaturated of all color. Then the image was opened in the app "Lo-Mob" and the 30s Contact 2 look applied to the image to create the feeling of a contact print from an old glass negative (remember negatives?). Finally the image was altered one last time in the app "Light Leak".

With the iPhone in hand, I seek out what inspires me most, the human form and texture. Each app, with its variety of effects, enhances, refines, and gives new emotion to the image.

The photo was taken using the app "Camera Genius", opened and filtered in the app "Impression", then altered further in the app "Abstractions". The final stage is to frame the piece in the app "FotoMuse".

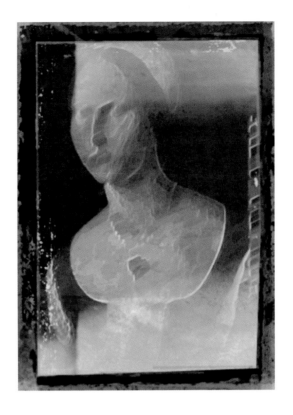

The portrait of the woman was shot with the iPhone app "Camera Genius". The image is opened in the app "ezimba" to give the image a painterly effect, then opened in "Photo Finish" to create a rough texture that creates the visual illusion of 3D paint peeling off an old wall.

I was born and raised in Berkeley, CA, surrounded by creativity. Both my parents and my sisters are artists and we were immersed in all manner of creative media. My previous art was mainly drawings using fine ink pens, detailed surreal images with tons of color. I currently live by the San Francisco Bay.

SOPHIA BY THE SEA

This was a great shot to begin with. No cropping. Processed in the app "Vintage Scene", and then I increased the color saturation of the dress in "Photo fx".

The Journey

BY MAIA PANOS
Artist
California, USA

The journey is filled with twists and turns where art flows and sometimes it doesn't. The artist's rekindled spark to creativity can be traced directly to her iPhone and app store.

STEPPING OUT

Her name is Angle. She loved the camera. I used "Pic Grunger" for texture, softened the background with "BlurFX" and popped the color of her comb using "Photo fx".

ROSE AWAKENING

I love flowers. I changed the color in the center of the rose in "Photo fx" and did a little sharpening. Finally, I added some texture in "Pic Grunger".

COMPANION

I arranged these calla lilies against a wall, processed the image in the app "Vintage Scene", then increased saturation of the flowers in "Photo fx".

KID IN HAY

I really enjoy taking photos of animals. This was another great shot. I did very little apping: processed in "Vintage Scene", softened background with "BlurFX".

My early influences were Mercer Mayer, best known for his illustrations of children's books; Brian Froud, whose drawings combined photographic realism with the magical world of mythical beings; Michael Parkes for his imagery; Gerhard Richter whose work is an awe-inspiring range in beautiful creations.

I took a long hiatus from my art, for various reasons. It was the iPhone which led to the reawakening of my creative spirit. With the iPhone in my pocket, I began taking pictures again and each new app creates a new path to creating artistic images with my photographs.

BAR

This photo was taken in Portland, Oregon. I opened the photo in the app "BlurFX", blurred the background, and then increased the saturation in "Photo fx".

WHAT A TANGLED WEB WE WEAVE

This photo is heavily apped. I blurred the background with the app "BlurFX", "Plastic Bullet" created the intense color and "Pic Grunger" added texture.

The iPhone is always with me and it allows me to capture the moments I would have missed otherwise.With the right applications and a little imagination, I can edit photos on the phone to create really artistic photographs, then share them with the world in a matter of minutes.

I most enjoy shooting textures, abstract objects, and lifestyle (photo journalistic) portraits.

"CameraBag" is my "go to" app, here set to Holga filter, giving the photo a square crop to isolate the flower and a vignette to help it stand out from the surrounding leaves.

Personal Vision Shared

BY TONY CECE
Photographer, Video Producer, Artist
Virginia, USA

Photographer/video producer Tony Cece finds the time to create his own brand of iPhone art, and share it with the rest of the world via photo-sharing groups.

JUST MARRIED

Unable to get in closer to my friends as they took their first dance, I imagined a different way to create an interesting shot. Most of my black-and-white images are shot using different "Hipstamatic" film packs; this one is BlacKeys SuperGrain. I then opened it in "Instagram" to add a tilt-shift effect, tint the image, and share it to my social media outlets.

MEDAN BELIZE, HAITI

Twelve photos were taken and assembled using "AutoStitch" to make this panorama of Lake Azuei. I added a gradient to bring color to the sky in "Photo fx" and made basic adjustments to the contrast in "Photogene" to make the colors pop.

A lot of my influences come from the movie/film industry. Most of my knowledge of photography is an adaptation of technical aspects I learned in film school. I loved the work that Gregg Toland did as the director of photography (DP) for Citizen Kane *and Gordon Willis did for* Godfather 1 *and* 2. *My favorite photographers are Jeremy Cowart, Esther Havens, and Chase Jarvis.*

NYC SKYLINE

A thirteen-photo "AutoStitch" of a nearly colorless NYC skyline was pulled into "Photo fx" to add color to the scene and give the appearance of sunrise.

ORLANDO SITS ON A BIKE RIM IN LAKE AZUEI WHILE MEN FROM THE VILLAGE FISH IN THE DISTANCE

This was taken in Haiti on a trip where I was using "Hipstamatic" as my main iPhone camera. This used the Blanko film and John S lens.

INDUSTRIAL WEEDS

After struggling with my digital SLR to create an image I liked at this location, I pulled out my iPhone to create this image. It was processed with "Pic Grunger" to blend a texture over the image and "Photogene" to brighten and add contrast.

I share my photos extensively on web-based sites like Flickr, Tumblr, Facebook, TwitPic, and my site, iPhonelomo.com. I have an iPhone Lomo specific group on the Flickr photo-sharing site that allows members to comment on aspects of each other's iPhone photos in an incredibly constructive and supportive way. Social media have opened up a world of creativity to me that I otherwise wouldn't have been able to be a part of. I enjoy the community of like minds as we come together and express ourselves and learn together.

DEAD SEA CALCIFICATION ON BRANCHES

Because of the starkness of this image and the water blending into the horizon, I decided to make the image black and white in "Photogene" and tinted it blue using the white balance to cool the image. "Camera+" was used to added clarity to the image and make the branches stand out.

DINO VS. THE TIGER

"Camera+" was used to add clarity and sharpness to stylize this image of my son looking at a tiger. Because the glass cannot be seen in this image, it appears as though my son is in the cage with the tiger. "Vignetting Camera" was used to darken the edges and draw attention to the subjects staring at each other.

California Dreaming

BY JOSE CHAVARRY
Artist
California, USA

Jose Chavarry's photographic vision is elegant and sophisticated, yet inspired by dreams and an infant's wide-eyed wonder.

My work is about dreams. I believe the way we process, problem-solve and structure our lives begins there …

Taking photos of everyday life and making them more surreal is my way of dreaming while I'm awake. I am constantly forcing myself to look at life in a new way, and as a result hoping to make different choices in my life that will make the world a more magical place.

Originally from Guatemala, I moved to Los Angeles when I was three years old. I have an MFA in Theatre from the University of California, San Diego, and live in Los Angeles, developing theatrical shows for a large healthcare organization.

THE FIRST DAY

This image was taken on the beach in Oceanside, California. I started by using the app "Iris Photo Suite" to saturate the colors with the HDR filter. I then processed the image using "BlurFX" to blur out everything except the figures on the sand. I finished processing the image by using "LensLight" to add some sun rays.

RUNAWAY PEACOCK

I shot this photo at a local arboretum. It was processed also using "Iris Photo Suite" to saturate and then "BlurFX" to isolate some details on the peacock. I also used "PhotoCopier" to add some texture to the image.

JOSE CHAVARRY
California Dreaming

DREAM OF SUMMER

This is part of a series of images that I called *Summer in Suburbia*, taken at a suburban park in San Diego. I grew up in the suburban tract homes outside Los Angeles. It was a very sterile, bland, but safe environment. I always remember feeling desperately bored during the summers. I suppose with this image and the series, I was trying to re-imagine an alternative childhood for myself. I used "BlurFX" to visually isolate the boy, "PhotoCopier" for texture, "LensLight" for light leaks, and "Iris Photo Suite" for color adjustments.

SO THE STORY GOES ...

This is a combination of two images I shot. One is a landscape of a park, and the images of people were from a photo I took at a train station. Using the app "Juxtaposer", I cut out and superimposed the people into the landscape. Unconsciously, I think I wanted to have them explore a new environment they would never be a part of: a dream world where they are all having the same dream. Then I used "BlurFX" to create focus only on the people and "Iris Photo Suite" to finetune the color palette and add some texture.

A lot of my images have been taken around train stations. I'm strangely drawn to them. For me, train stations are a metaphor for the place we are in just before our transition from conscious to unconscious.

WINTER TRACKS

This was taken at the Burbank Metro station. I don't typically process my images in black and white, but it was a particularly cold winter and I had been away from my wife and daughter for a few months. I shot this image after dropping them off at the station, blurring the scene except for the foreground tracks using the app "BlurFX" and then using the Vintage Scene setting in "PhotoCopier" to convey how I was feeling at the time.

THE DEARLY DEPARTED

This was taken at the trolley station in downtown San Diego. I wasn't sure whether the two people in the image had just been dropped off or were saying goodbye. I used "BlurFX" for isolating the two figures and then "FX Studio", "Iris Photo Suite", and "PictureShow" for color manipulation and some scratches.

My personal influences are Caravaggio, Bresson, David Lynch, Terry Gilliam, and Rothko. The common thread? The artists who influence me the most always seek truth, but sometimes have to distort "reality" in order to find it.

In the best scenario, my images have a magical effect on the viewer—if not consciously, then perhaps at night when they dream.

I like the quote from a Haruki Murakami book, Sputnik Sweetheart. He writes, "I dream. Sometimes I think it's the only right thing to do."

I have always been imaginative, immersing myself in the art of music, video and photography. With the iPhone, it introduced me to the world of instant art. Inspired by the beauty of God's creation, life, and art, I capture everyday objects and manipulate them into something different, giving them a fresh perspective. When I see something that interests me, I try to break down all the different components and recreate it. Mistakes are okay, since without them we couldn't improve. "

When I see something that interests me I try to break down all the different components and re-create it. Mistakes are okay, since without them we couldn't improve.

RETRO TVS

I came across these old TVs so I used the apps "CameraBag" and "Mill Colour" to create the vintage look of photography when these TVs were new. First I ran it through "CameraBag" using the 1962 setting and then I adjusted it in "Mill Colour" with the 1970s filter to get the sepia tone.

BIG RED

Longest door I've ever seen. I took the picture into "PhotoCurves" and adjusted the RGB curves to give it that cross-processing look. I finished the image in "Mill Colour" with the Promo filter to make the colors pop.

Eloquent Altered Photos

BY ALEX ACEVEDO
Photographer, Designer,
Musician
Colorado, USA

Alex Acevedo combines his eye for photography with a collection of apps that help transform his images into a more expressive body of work.

BLIND EYES

Some great light from the rising sun came through my blinds. I blended that photo with a self-portrait in the app "DXP", using the Soft Light setting, and then adjusted the contrast with curves in "PhotoCurves".

The iPhone has been revolutionary in bringing a studio to your pocket. You can take a picture and allow your creativity to work right then and there with all the different apps, instead of waiting until later or forgetting about the idea you had. The iPhone may not have the best camera, but this proves it's not all about the camera you use but the creativity you bring to it.

ARBOL DE FUEGO

Sometimes I walk my dog before the sun comes up and this one time I found the sunrise hitting these trees. It looked so beautiful. I used "Snapseed" to intensify the sunlight to look as if the branches were on fire.

WAITING FOR CHRISTMAS

My wife was counting the days till we went to Miami to see our family for Christmas. I tried to communicate that with this double exposure I created in "DXP". Then I took it into "Snapseed" to adjust the colors.

NIGHT SWIRLS

The photo was taken at night and swirled during the exposure. With the long shutter exposure in dark lighting conditions, the iPhone allows you to write with light. I then saturated the colors using "PhotoCurves".

STOP AND SHOOT

I opened the photo in "Mill Colour" and applied the Promo filter to increase the contrast and create the cyan tint.

TANNING BY THE POOL

I've always been a fan of Lomography™ cameras. This was my attempt at replicating that. We blend two photos in "DXP" and use "PhotoCurves" to give it the cross-processed look.

Evocative Photography

BY SEAN SHERIDAN
Photographer, Gaffer
New York, USA

Sean and Lucy Sheridan both have a love of image-making and some interesting iPhone apps that include the concepts of time and place. They share their thoughts and techniques for making their personal art on the iPhone.

Sean Sheridan is a photographer and a gaffer/lighting director in the motion picture industry. Sean has been publishing his photographs on the web since 2002 on his personal website and on various photo-sharing networks.

One of my favorite apps is "ToyCamera", used here with an image taken of a spoon in a French café at night. The way "ToyCamera" renders the highlights, crushes the blacks, and reflects the existing color balance really adds to the sense of "place" in this photo.

SEAN SHERIDAN
Evocative Photography

"QuadCamera" lets you capture four pictures into a grid within a short period of time. You're forced to visualize your four exposures into a final composition on the spot, although the app allows you to control the length of the delay between exposures to up to thirty seconds.

"QuadCamera" applies vignettes in contrast to the corners of each of the individual pictures, which creates a mysterious framing device. It introduces the fourth dimension, time, to the artwork and, when successful, manages to capture the essence of a place, to depict place in an exceptional way.

The app "ToyCamera" creates effects in a random way, which gives you a surprise every time you take a picture, not unlike the Lomo or Holga style of photography with the instant gratification of a Polaroid. It's fun and interactive. Here, "ToyCamera" was used to crop the image and add a vignette, helping to isolate and feature our subject.

My wife and I take turns taking pictures whenever we see something interesting, and we get amazingly different results.

Intuitive
Storytelling

BY LUCY SHERIDAN
Photographer, Production
Manager
New York, USA

Production manager and photographer Lucy Sheridan uses her iPhone to paint portraits of her favorite days sauntering around the city with her husband Sean Sheridan. Whether shooting in NYC or Paris, where she lived for eighteen years, Lucy uses her innate sense of aesthetics to create amazing artwork that captures time and place in an almost cinematic way. Here, she shares her thoughts on this less technical, more intuitive process.

What I love best about the iPhone camera is that it functions as a fun hobby to share with the people I love, peppering our days with something fun and memorable. My husband and I spent a very special Valentine's Day fixing a Polaroid camera, on which we made tons of instant memories. The iPhone provides the same instant satisfaction and delight, creating beautiful keepsakes in a way that is inexpensive and easy. Now we take even more pictures when the moment strikes.

It's a misconception that the various iPhone apps restrict a savvy photographer. For instance, my favorite app—"QuadCamera"—gives you only a few seconds to choose four frames. Not only does this improve composition skills, but this lack of time to think allows you to create something deeper and more intuitive. The app helps you develop this instinctual skill.

"QuadCamera" introduces the element of time into the process of photography. For the quad to work, the timing needs to be right. My comfort zone is two seconds—anything quicker and half the pictures come out blurry, anything slower and I get bored. It always takes me a few attempts to get the timing down—it's really simple but it takes a few tries to adjust your mind to thinking about the final composition created using four images. Just try it out and play with it. It's very satisfying.

Apps and Inspiration

BY MICHAEL GAROFALO

Photographer, Assistant
Cameraman, Musician
New York, USA

Michael Garofalo describes
his evolution into iPhone
photography, and details the
steps and apps used to create
his photographic art.

Born and raised in Fresh Meadows, Queens, NY. I went to the School of Visual Arts in NYC to study Film and Photography. After college, I learned motion picture camera equipment while working at a rental house and went on to become a union motion picture camera assistant. I've worked with every kind of professional camera, from stills to motion picture to the latest HiDef. My personal camera of choice ... the iPhone.

I opened the image of Kevin Burke in the app "Polarize" to crop it into the old SX-70 format. I saved it to the camera roll, then opened the result in the app "Photogene" to change color balance, saturation, and exposure, finishing the image with the puzzle effect in the app "Vihgo".

I shot a photo in the app "QuadCamera" in the Hi-con mode to pump up the contrast and brought the result into the app "Polarize" to get the SX-70 cropping. Then the image was finished off in the app "Vihgo" by adding the rain effect.

The photo is opened in the app "FocalLab" and given a slight diffusion effect, then finished in the app "Mill Colour" using the Print Look setting.

I opened the photo in "Polarize" for the SX-70 format, then in the app "Photogene" to increase color saturation. I finished the image with a soft focus vignette using the app "FocalLab".

The most important aspect of my iPhone camera is availability—the opportunity to photograph anything, any time.

There is a constant evolution when you are dealing with iPhone apps. I have my favorites, but there is always a new app on the horizon that can change the way I create my art. Then when I'm done with the image, I can send it around the world with one click of a button. This has to be one of the greatest joys in my life. It's always a great feeling to express yourself through photography, but now you can share that feeling with the rest of the world instantly.

The photo (right) was opened in the app "Photo fx", where I applied a warm tint and adjusted the color temperature, Then the Holga Vignette effect was added in the app "Camera-Bag" to complete the image.

The photo (top far right) was opened in the app "Mill Colour" and I applied the Print Look effect to the image. I opened the result in the app "Photogene" to increase the saturation, decrease the exposure, and add a frame. A slight tint was then added in the app "Photo fx" to finish the piece.

The photo was opened in the app "Photogene", where the contrast was increased to isolate the illuminated window and the tape was added to the corners.

This early morning image was opened in the app "Photogene", where the contrast and color saturation were increased to create the dramatic sky. The result was opened in the app "FocalLab" to apply an overall diffusion that finalizes the image.

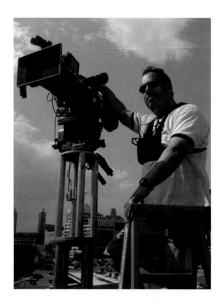

Cartooning on the iPhone

BY MICHAEL GAROFALO
Photographer, Assistant
Cameraman, Musician
New York, USA

Michael Garofalo loves to tell a story, and with the apps "ToonPAINT" and "Strip Designer" he seems to have found a new vehicle. Here he shows us how it's done.

I start with four original iPhone photos, which in turn are opened in the app "ToonPAINT". Slider controls allow you to control details and the levels of black, gray, and white that make up the cartoon version of the photograph. Advanced options are also available to achieve some varied looks to the final cartoon. All results are then saved to the camera roll.

Depending on the story or the design, some cartoon images are brought into the app "DXP" to add color. Below, the original photo and the "ToonPAINT" version are composited using the Luminosity setting to achieve the look of the third image. The result is saved to the camera roll.

SAVE	Settings	APPLY
COMPOSITE EFFECT		
HALFMIX		
MULTIPLY		
SCREEN		
OVERLAY		
SOFTLIGHT		
HARDLIGHT		
DIFFERENCE		
COLOR		
LUMINOSITY		✓
EXCLUSION		

The comic strip designer always begins with a great story. Then the photos of characters, objects, and locations are prepared, as illustrated on the opposite page.

Open the app "Strip Designer" and choose your template from a multitude of choices provided within the app.

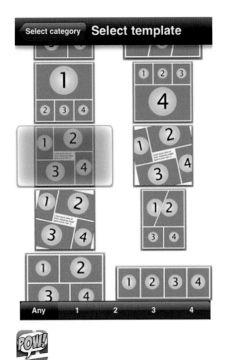

The cartoon's elements are then placed into the template. Images can now be resized and rotated inside each box of the chosen template. Once I finish positioning the elements inside the template, I move to the textbox section. Select the type of text balloon (or thought bubble), then add, position, and resize the balloon where you want it. Now it's time to add the dialogue to the balloon. Repeat the process for all the frames shown until the cartoon strip is finished.

App Stacking
Artistry

BY CINDY PATRICK
Artist, Photographer
New Jersey, USA

Schooled in alternative photographic processes, mobile devices and the App store have allowed this artist to create without hesitation. Well known in the iPhone art community, here she demonstrates the use of multiple apps to arrive at her eloquent visual destinations.

I was born, raised and still live and work in south/central New Jersey, just over the bridge from Philadelphia. I am a professional photographer, shooting mostly weddings and portraits in conjunction with creating my personal art. When I went away to college and discovered photography, I became interested in alternative processes and the manipulated photograph—toning, hand-coloring, liquid emulsions, etc. Anything to alter the image in some way. I eventually discovered Polaroid materials—image and emulsion transfers and SX-70 manipulated photos—and I was hooked!

What attracted and excited me the most about Polaroid was the instantaneous nature of the materials and processes. Now with the iPhone, iPad, and the enormous array of apps available, that magic has returned for me! One hundred percent of my personal work is now shot with my iPhone.

SOLITUDE

I captured the original scene using "Classic PAN" to achieve the panoramic format. I then brought the image into "Artista Sketch" and created a sketch of the scene. I layered the original image with the sketch in "Iris Photo Suite" and adjusted the color using the WWII filter. I then opened "Diptic" and selected a three-window layout. Normally, you would put three different images into the three window panes, but here I put the same image into the three panes and adjusted them until I was satisfied with the way the edges matched up. Finally, I took the triptych into "King Camera" and added the "grunge" texture.

GREAT CONCENTRATION IS REQUIRED TO CATCH PLASTIC FISH

I captured the original image using the "Native iPhone 4 Camera". I cropped it square using "Photoshop Express" to eliminate some distracting elements. Two layers were required to make the final image. To create the first layer, I took the original into "BlurFX" and blurred everything except the boys. For the second layer, I took the original into "AutoPainter II" and created a sketch of the scene using the Felt Tip setting. The two layers were then brought into "Iris Photo Suite", where they were blended using the Soft Light setting. Finally, I applied a grunge filter to add some texture (this was the Old Wood filter).

I am drawn predominantly to nature, the landscape, city and suburban street scenes, and the beach. I have a series called Beach Memoirs *which has really attracted a lot of attention, so I plan to do a lot more of that and keep the series going.*

I have become a regular contributor to P1xels (pixelsatanexhibition.com), which is another wonderful community of incredibly talented iPhoneographers. I have had several of my images published there and have received "The Daily Pic" five times. P1xels accepted one of my images into a recent iPhoneography exhibition at the Giorgi Gallery in Berkeley, California, and my image appears on the cover of the exhibition catalog, an incredible thrill and honor!

IN QUIET WATERS

I captured the original scene using "Classic PAN" to achieve the panoramic format. Two layers were required to make the final image. To create the first layer, I took the original into "BlurFX" and blurred the entire scene, erasing part of the blur in the grass to allow some detail to show through. For the second layer, I took the original into "Artista Sketch" and created a sketch of the scene. The two layers were then brought into "Iris Photo Suite" where they were blended using the Soft Light setting. I then applied a grunge filter to add some texture (this was the Old Wood filter). The image was then brought into "Vintage Scene" to give it an antiqued look and to add the border effect.

WHERE DO I BEGIN?

This is a self-portrait, something that's rare for me, but fun to do on occasion! I captured the original using the "Native iPhone 4 Camera". I first took the image into "BlurFX" to blur out the background and to soften all of my facial features except my eyes. I then brought the image into "Decim8" and simply played around with the random settings until I achieved something I liked. (That's often how I use "Decim8", although you have full control over the settings.) I then took the image into "Filter Mania" (which crops the image into a square) and applied the Grunge filter to finish it off.

AT PHARAOH'S GATE

This was actually a fairly simple one to create. I captured this image at a carnival at night using "Slow Shutter". I took the original into "AutoPainter II" and made a sketch of it using the Felt Tip setting. Finally, I brought the image into "Iris Photo Suite" and applied a grunge filter.

WHILST WAVES MARKED TIME

This was a combination of three images I shot using the "Slow Shutter" app. I brought each image individually into "Lo-Mob" and added the slide border effect to each one. Lastly, I combined them into a triptych using the "Diptic" app.

I have been influenced and inspired throughout my life by painters such as Cézanne, Monet, Chagall, Hopper, and many modern watercolorists, and photographers such as Keith Carter, Sylvia Plachy, William Eggleston, Henri Cartier-Bresson, Rocky Schenk, Helen Levitt, Sam Abell, William Albert Allard, Robert Doisneau, and Robert Frank, to name a few. When I first discovered iPhoneography, Chase Jarvis and Dan Marcolina were huge influences.

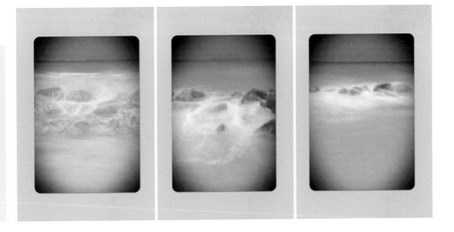

Multi-App Magic

CINDY PATRICK
Artist, Photographer
New Jersey, USA

As an artist, I've always been much more interested in making images than taking photographs. My passion is for creating images that express how I feel about a subject rather than depicting the world around me in a purely representational way.

Rooms with a View *is what mobile artists call a mash-up. Since apps have unique functionality, mash-up artists move an image or variations of an image to multiple apps to accomplish things normally reserved for "Photoshop" users.*

STEP 1

I started with two iPhone photos: the main photo, a shot of some buildings from a hotel window in New York City, and another of two birds on a wire.

STEP 2

I brought the photo of the buildings into "BlurFX" and blurred everything, erasing the blur in some places to reveal the windows.

STEP 3

I then brought that image into "Image Blender", and blended it with the image of the birds.

STEP 4

I then brought that image into "Artista Sketch" and made a monochromatic grungy textured sketch of it.

STEP 5

I brought the images from Steps 3 and 4 into "Iris Photo Suite" and layered them together using the Soft Light blending mode.

STEP 6

I then brought the image into Tiffen's "Photo fx Ultra" and added a blue grad filter to the sky to add some drama.

STEP 7

Next, I brought the image into "PhotoCopier" and applied the Klee filter to give some texture to the buildings, taking the image into the realm of Klee's imagery.

STEP 8

I brought the images from Steps 5 and 6 into "Iris Photo Suite" and layered them, which allowed me to erase the Klee filter from the sky and window areas of the buildings, thus applying the Klee filter very selectively at varying opacity.

STEP 9

Next, I brought the image into "ScratchCamFX" and added some texture and adjusted the color to make it more saturated.

STEP 10

I then brought the image into "Weather Photo Effects", where I applied one of the Space filters.

STEP 11

Lastly, I brought the images from Steps 9 and 10 back into "Iris Photo Suite" and placed them on separate layers, which allowed me to erase the Space filter from everything except the sky.

I have a Bachelor's degree in Art, and I took lots and lots of photography courses to fulfill my major. I had some wonderful teachers, but I am by and large self-taught in many respects. When I want to learn something, I read books. I have an entire library of books on all sorts of photography-related topics—not just fine art photography books, of which I have dozens, but books ranging from the inspirational (David duChemin) to the technical (Joe McNally). For me, books will always be associated with learning.

I truly believe we are at the forefront of a movement that will some day find its place in the history of photography. Photography itself is a relatively young medium, and I think iPhoneography is now where photography was in the late 19th century and early 20th century, when photographers were attempting to validate it as an art form. Well, that argument has been settled, and I think eventually iPhoneography will have its own chapter written in the history books. Each of us is writing that history right now, with every single image posted, every single exhibit mounted, and every single article written. I am certain that we are witnessing the birth of a new art form.

I work on my iPhoneography every day. I tend to work and rework an image, trying a variety of different apps and combinations of apps until I feel it is finished. This could take anywhere from a couple of hours to a couple of months. I will often end up with several versions of a single image, and it's really tough sometimes to decide which one is the "keeper". I think that's one of the hardest things about being an artist, knowing when a piece is finished.

Base Drawing 1: 'LiveSketch'.

MAKING *NIGHT FLYER TINKERING*, WITH SOME SIDE DIVERSIONS

Drawing has a vitality that is hard to capture in other mediums. Simple drawing captures spontaneity and presents direct storytelling that can touch our emotions more than any other medium, except maybe music. A drawing with brush and ink, once committed to paper, is unforgiving. Digital drawing, on the other hand, is very forgiving, with undo and duplicate commands at the touch of the fingers. This is a boon when you don't map out or plan what the final image should look like. I had quickly adapted to working within the small screen of the iPhone and experienced its intimacy as a 'drawing medium'. The iPad changed everything, becoming my clear favourite artmaking device.

TIP Frequently, one drawing evolves into different stand-alone drawings by being mashed or rehashed into a completely different image.

STEP 1

I make a quick series of sketches chasing an idea until it takes shape and has some meaning to me. The app 'LiveSketch' was used for the two base drawings, then merged in the app 'DXP' using the Multiply setting. This is the start of *Propeller Head*, *Icarus* and the *Night Flyer* series.

Night Flyer Tinkering

BY JULIAN WIGLEY
Architect, Artist
Darwin, Northern Territory,
Australia

This artist's background with traditional and digital media comes full circle with the iPhone and iPad firmly fitted in his toolbox. This tutorial will take us on his journey through multiple apps and stunning multiple final results.

JULIAN WIGLEY
Collage and Paint Mash-Up Master

STEP 1A

Opportunities arise: the first side drawing happens: *Propeller Head*. 'ToonPAINT' added texture and the drawing was mashed with colour photos using 'DXP'.

Base Drawing 2. 'LiveSketch'.

Propeller Head.

Base Drawing, 'LiveSketch'.

Mashed with this lion's head (a discarded dry gully).

STEP 2

I worked on the original black-and-white sketch further by mashing it with other drawings using 'DXP' and importing it into 'Brushes' for the iPad, which allows for unsurpassed control over layered painting. This is looking for an image—the chase. There is no thought of the flyer, just a man's profile. This head was developed into the stand-alone drawing *Icarus*.

Icarus

The above two images were combined in 'DXP' using the Soft Light setting.

Reworked with 'Brushes'.

The reworking is mashed further using 'DXP' and background photos, until it's time to stop. That is, I have an image that has meaning to me: *Icarus*.

STEP 3

Icarus is combined with the first 'LiveSketch' drawing using 'DXP'. I added some details using 'Brushes' to delineate the head and the propeller after the mash. *Icarus* turns back into the pilot. There is now colour and tone.

STEP 4

The pilot's torso is derived from the image below and composited in 'Brushes'. The images of gears are sized, positioned and layered into the headgear. The 'Brushes' app for the iPad allows positioning and scale commands when importing a drawing. I put each drawing on a separate layer for additional control with opacity settings and brushwork.

Another side drawing happens—the *Night Flyer* series. The aeroplane cockpit is a photo mash, using 'DXP', of a tablecloth taken in Tuscany, a jumble of computer cables taken in Darwin and a photo of clouds in my photo library. The pilot is composited into the piece using 'Brushes for iPad', resulting in the *Night Flyer* series.

STEP 5

Raid your library for elements to combine into a new image.

A tablecloth from Tuscany was used as the cockpit. I used 'Brushes for iPad' to manipulate elements by putting them on separate layers, shifting their position and painting them together.

This drawing illustrates the joy of mobile digital art—it would take me several hours to produce some of the complexity found in parts of this image, whereas it has been made with some ease and in reasonable time by using this new tool. And, being digital, the image remains for further experiment, exploration and manipulation.

Gears for headgear, above, at a low opacity.

The torso and left arm from my drawing *Pajama Man* are selected and manipulated in 'Brushes' to make the pilot.

Influences—first off, my father, the painter James V. Wigley, and my mother, who told me to get a real job. Da Vinci's machines and drawings, Le Corbusier (his drawings), Rembrandt, Goya, Käthe Kollwitz, Hogarth, George Cruikshank, Degas, Saul Steinberg and George Grosz, to name a few.

Night Flyer

THE DIGITAL COLLAGE—FINALISING OF *NIGHT FLYER TINKERING*

STEP 6

The pilot was scaled up and mashed with another abstract drawing (letter A) to provide a background. The final image takes shape.

TIP For pure variety of the visual possibilities of combining images, I prefer the flexibility and filter range of the app 'DXP'. But 'Brushes for iPad' lets you manipulate an imported image, where you can shrink, enlarge, rotate and position a new layer before accepting it within the collage. Once accepted, the opacity of the layer can then be adjusted or you can erase parts using the eraser. Best of all are some layer-merging settings to change the way that each layer interacts with others, and the ability to merge and combine layers. When I create an image using multiple layers and want to keep merging and adding layers, this feature allows me to build up a dense final composite.

STEP 7

The overall drawing is shaped using paint as an eraser, adding details with brushes and combining a mash-up from my library—a logo and a steering wheel from an old Humber Snipe. Each is placed on its own layer and painted into the final composite.

STEP 8

Final touches. The background is reworked to make it less ambiguous. Some ideas are sketched out directly on the image, in search of an elegant end: finally, deciding on pasting in the *Night Flyer* head and torso, on top of its own scaled-up image, then adding the hand holding the tools. The A was turned into a ladder. The medium allows you to work quickly when chasing down an idea.

My work is usually representational, looking for the satirical edge without falling over it. Mediums include brush/pen and ink, pastel, and all wet mediums; occasional comic publishing; and the odd animation using sand, pastel and graphite and some digital work. Now I've added my mobile devices to the workflow.

Electronic fingerpainting is an intimate experience. The directness of making marks, the immediacy of accessing stored images, the ease of creating new textures, patterns and colours, and, most of all, being freed from the desktop computer, draws me to the iPad. I see it as a printing press, where along with the myriad intuitive applications, I can make, mix, match, mash and publish images ... and it's much smaller than my Gutenberg.

The current mobile art applications are not 'bloated' and all seem compatible on the iPad and iPhone. They provide a level of control as well as offering surprises by experiment, something you would expect from a tool for making art.

Postscript

The medium allows tremendous freedom in making pictures, little or big, that can emulate traditional mediums or forge new visual languages. The software available is straightforward and does not get in the way of our hands and eyes when we make our pictures.

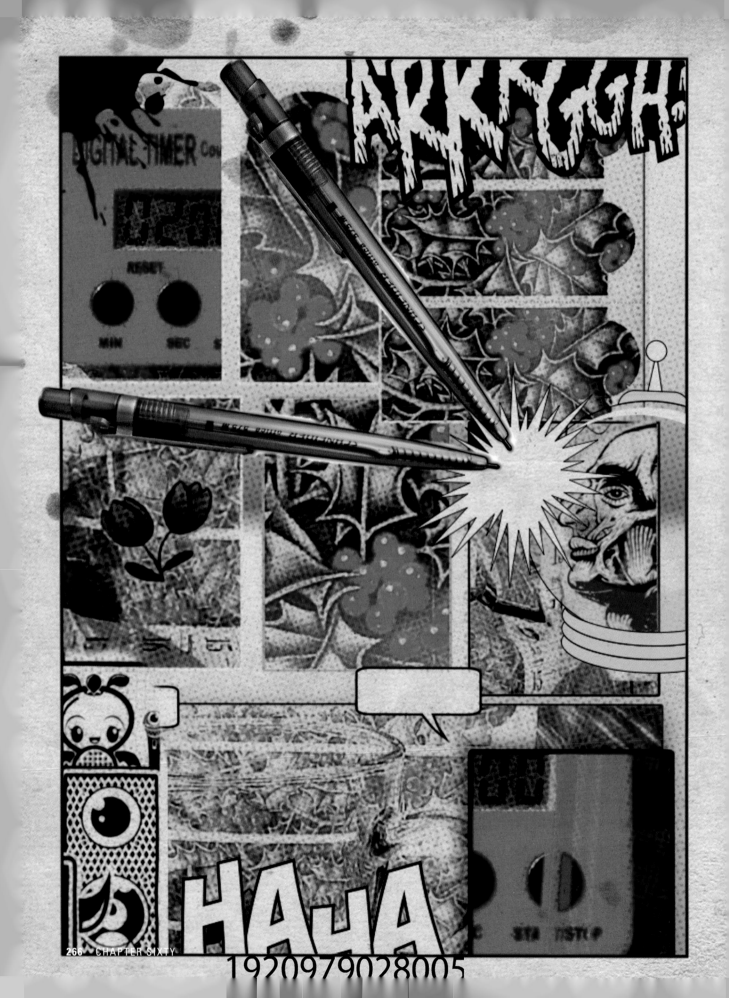

With my iPad, my work became more free, less formal. Less about technique but more about content. Suddenly I needed to say something or to comment or to tell funny stories, and anything is possible.

The apps I used to create this piece: "Pixlr-o-matic", "Halftone", "Comic Life", "Painterly" and "Photoshop Touch".

Original iPad Photo.

Dreamt on Demand

BY JAN UITERWIJK
Artist, Cartographer
The Netherlands

After a lifetime of creating maps and intricate drawings for a living, Jan Uiterwijk is now retired and free to make art on his iPad that makes his spirit soar.

I opened the original photo in the app "Pixlr-o-matic" to isolate this section of the picture and then saved it.

The art I make on the iPad is mainly collages or graphic related art. And I'm a comic addict and try to do something related with comics, but not as a comic ...

A second photo was opened in "Pixlr-o-matic" to add the neon stripe. This too was saved to the camera roll.

To create this collage, I used the app "Comic Life". It allows me to choose a template and then add my various saved elements for my first pass at this composite. I can resize and reposition each element as I add it. This allows me to use pieces of the same elements to compose this collage, creating a strong visual harmony.

I switched to the app "Painterly" to add the head and the element at lower left. "Painterly" is a kind of "transfer paint" app. Take a target from the camera roll and paint a part or the entire source into your art. These parts came from other elements I created and had saved in the photo library of my iPad.

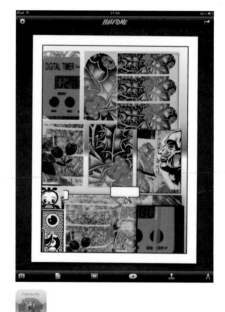

I'm a big fan of the app "Halftone", so I imported the sources in "Halftone" and added textures and borders.

Still in "Comic Life", I added empty balloons to a few areas of the collage.

I switched back to the app "Halftone" to crop and add text, the inkspot at upper left and the green helmet.

Still in the app "Halftone", I added a wonderful weathered paper called O Positive as a background to the piece.

I imported the green pen file into the app "Photoshop Touch", duplicated the layer and repositioned both the pens, shown at right, to finish the piece.

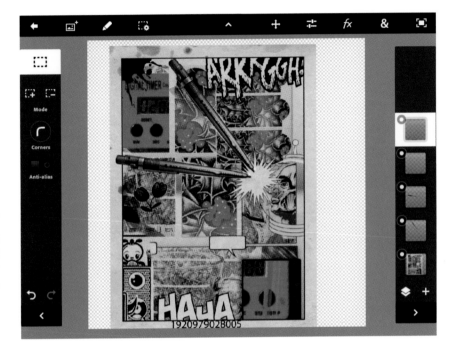

Some of my favorite artists are David Hockney, Raoul Dufy, Aat Verhoog, Pat Andrea, Dürer, and Holbein. But influenced? I don't know … that's for someone else to say …

I live in the western part of the Netherlands, in a small town. I'm now retired but was a mapmaker / cartographer for forty-seven years. A photographer since I was sixteen years old, I've created thousands of photographs and artworks, maps and drawings, all without formal art education. I'm a self-made artist and I love to read.

I share my work in Flickr, where it is now possible to communicate and interact with fellow artists all over the world.

Original Photo.

STEP 1

I opened the app "123D Sculpt" and imported the portrait into the apps photo library. Using the Image Rub tool, I positioned the head model to line up with the photo and "painted" the photo onto the model.

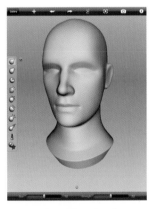

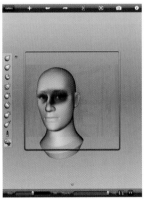

123D Sculpt" Screenshots.

Forced Perspective

BY BEN OSHMAN

Artist, Art Director, Propmaster
New Jersey, USA

Working in the flim industry, especially in the art department, expands your thinking to include set pieces, and how to create illusions. This thinking inspires me to create unlikely visual environments and fill them with unlikely components. The iPhone, iPad and the multitude of photo/art apps makes visualization of ideas a matter of inspiration, the tools are right there.

BEN OSHMAN
Forced Perspective

STEP 2

I rotated the 3D model to the final position and saved the file without a background to the camera roll.

Original iPhone Photographs.

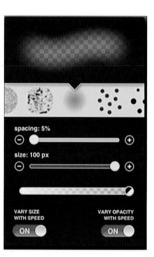

STEP 3

I opened both images above in the app "Brushes" on separate layers. Using a large soft eraser, I created a perfect blend of the images by erasing the top portion of the tracks image to reveal the city and sky on the layer below.

Blended in "Brushes".

"Brushes" Screenshots.

STEP 4

I brought the saved file from "123D Sculpt" into "Brushes", resized it, and positioned it as shown.

STEP 5

To finish the piece, I brought the original photo into "Brushes" on another layer, resized and repositioned it to overlay the 3D portrait and painted pieces of it back in using a soft brush at a low opacity. I restored her neck, hair, and half of her face, leaving an eerie portrait that subliminally reinforces the forced perspective and feeling of depth and dimension.

Experimentation
Perseverance Art

BY IQUANYIN MOON
Artist, Photographer
Hawaii, USA

Iquanyin gives her iPhone a workout and runs her ideas through multiple visual permutations before picking just the right one to show the world.

I've been an artist, singer, book editor, animal trainer, manual laborer, street performer, relationship astrologer, caregiver, portrait painter, and more. I'm a longtime Buddhist, and I love Oahu.

The photo was taken with the app "ToyCamera", then I opened the image in "Mill Colour", where I used the Bleached filter to give the original photo its desaturated look.

IQUANYIN MOON
Experimentation Perseverance Art

The photo was run through several filter apps so I have a library of variations to work with. Apps used: "Filter Mania", "Camera+", "Awesomer", and "Mill Colour". ("Filter Mania" and "Camera+" are current equivalents for free photo filter apps used to create some variations, but that are no longer in the App Store.) All results were saved to the camera roll.

The original and a few filtered variations were run through the app "Polarize", and the variations were saved to the camera roll.

Using "Mobile Safari", I found a great graphic and saved it to my iPhone camera roll. I ran the graphic through the app "Photo Lab" twice, once to remove color and make it a line drawing, once to give it a textured, embossed effect.

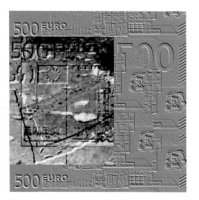

My main inspiration is love of form and experimentation. The intensity of my life demands expression, and images are my chosen voice for that. Artists who've inspired me include Matisse, Robert Mapplethorpe, and Kandinsky, to name a few.

Using the app "DXP", I created various versions of the polarized and full-sized images layered together using "DXP"'s many effects, and saved the variations to my camera roll.

I layered various combinations of filtered versions on other filtered versions and saved them. I kept layering versions on other versions, adding back the original if it got too faint, adding a semi-opaque version (the Exclusion effect in "DXP") or just a lighter version (the Screen effect in "DXP") if things started getting too dark.

I kept working the image, layering, trying different effects and combinations in "DXP" until there were several finished versions. I layered the modified web graphic once, early on, since I wanted it for "seasoning" the image, not as the entrée. The final version selected, *Girl with the White Tail*, is shown below.

TIP Use screenshots of text messages or notes, and make a translucent drawing to add depth to the image.

Collage/Tableaux Using Altered Photos and Prose

BY CHRISTINE FINKELSON
Photographer, Artist
California, USA

Christine Finkelson documents the small visual moments of her life with her iPhone and then, using her iPhone, iPad, and a variety of apps, combines these elements into a personal emotional tableaux.

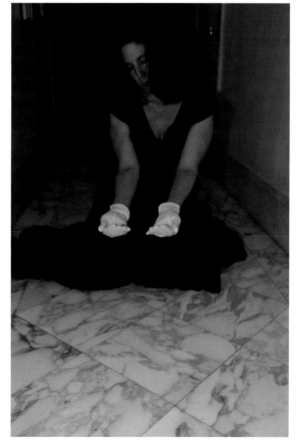

THE MAKING OF THE PIECE
LIFE IN SHATTERS: STEP 1

Using a photo I shot with my iPhone, I opened the woman with the gloves image in the app "TiltShift Generator", creating a dreamlike focus. The result was saved to the camera roll.

STEP 2

A picture of piano keys was opened in the app "Photogene", an app chock full of image controls, where it was converted to grayscale, the contrast and brightness were adjusted, and it was then saved to the camera roll.

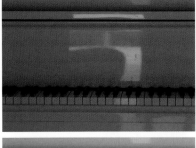

STEP 3

In the app "TypeDrawing", a unique app that paints with text, I opened a background image and then entered the prose below into the app. You then paint with words, with speed sensitivity to control font size as you paint. The resulting element (above) was saved to the camera roll.

STEP 4

I photographed a loose arrangement of a few of my old photos and opened the result in the "CameraBag" app where the Fisheye tab was used to create a circular object, and then saved it to the camera roll.

STEP 5

The tree image was opened in the app "Juxtaposer", this photo becoming our background. The woman image from Step 1 was imported into the top layer and flipped, and using the eraser tool I erased around the outline of her body to reveal more of the background.

This is the content of the prose, painted in Step 3 left:

My head is filled with art; I'm handing over my beloved apartment; there is a female warrior hovering over my shoulder; it's the holidays but I have no tree so in the background is a bare tree; there are so many words. swirling around in a void where the unknown lies.

STEP 6

Still in "Juxtaposer", I opened the text image from Step 3, erased around the text and used the fader within the app to give it a transparency of 75 percent, so you can still see some trees from the background layer.

STEP 7

The circle layer from Step 4 was opened in "Juxtaposer", cut out using the eraser tool and positioned over the woman's head. The piano was then imported, cut, resized, and positioned.

STEP 8

Lastly, a previous creation was imported and placed at the top left corner of the piece and resized, and the final version was saved to the camera roll.

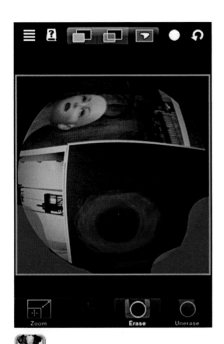

I was coming home on the train from a Thanksgiving meal in Philadelphia. I was thinking how much my life is shifting into a whole new level. I have been very prolific lately with my art and photography. However, I am now disassembling my life in Manhattan preparing a move to the west coast. My husband and I have been living in George Gershwin's old apartment for twelve years and we have just sold it. So I just spontaneously created this piece with all those emotions swirling around.

Life in Shatters sounds negative, but to me it's just the disconnected that will eventually come back together. Lastly, I had just seen a Duchamp exhibit at the Philadelphia Art Museum and was feeling positive about the possibilities of things being shattered and then put back together, with new meaning.

Essential apps on my mobile devices give me the power to always have a Holga camera, a tilt and shift lens, a Polaroid camera, and a multitude of "Photoshop"-type applications. I've already created a series, now in my portfolio, that was created on the iPhone. I've blown them up and printed them on 17 x 22 inch Hahnemühle fine art paper and fine art printable metal sheets. The textures and look are exactly what I was hoping for when conceiving the pictures.

The experience for me working with the iPhone and iPad to create photographic collages is equivalent to jazz music. In fact many times I'm listening to some jazz while I'm creating a piece. Whenever I see an interesting texture, line, light, or subject I will snap a photograph with my iPhone, knowing that I can use these in the future or for a current piece of work. They are like musical riffs that I play upon and collage, putting together an idea or feeling.

Taking what's been on my mind that is interesting me or concerning me jump-starts a piece. I begin with a background picture or color that represents my feeling at the moment. I then fit, retrofit, erase, morph the images and collage them with more of an intuitive manner than a deliberate manner. I let something serendipitous take over, and much of the time that leads to another riff and then a visual gift. At times an entire photograph can be reduced to just a sliver—only I know what it is and it lends a balance to the piece with a bit of mystery. Carbon Scare is a meditation on potential breast cancer. The lumps, the exams, the mammogram, the woman's body, beliefs, and prayers are all compartmentalized into boxes.

New Moon, below, was created during a new moon. I was feeling the magic of the moon and how it affects life. The energy of the moon influences people, the oceans, and thus the skies.

Opposite page: A Healing Dream was created for an organization that deals with women who have been abused. It was donated for these women in celebration of their courage and healing.

There is a renascent art that has been created by an arsenal of artistic applications (apps). Artists of all different mediums have experimented and created amazing pieces of art on their mobile devices. We now have the freedom to create wherever and whenever we desire and all our tools fit right into one hand. Imagine—no, better yet, experience—collaborating with another artist across the globe! It cannot be denied that this is indeed a new art form. The most thrilling aspect of all this for me is that it's just the beginning.

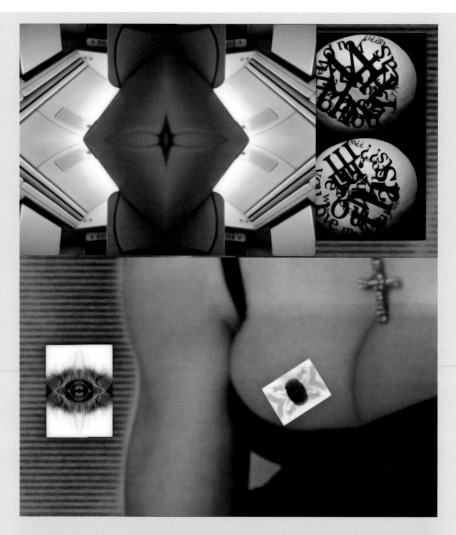

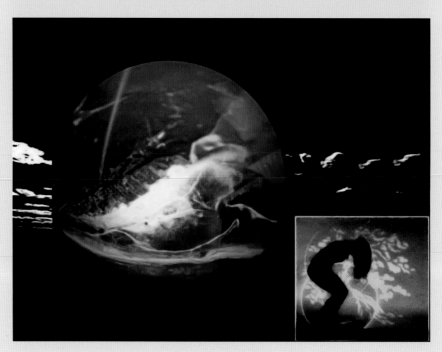

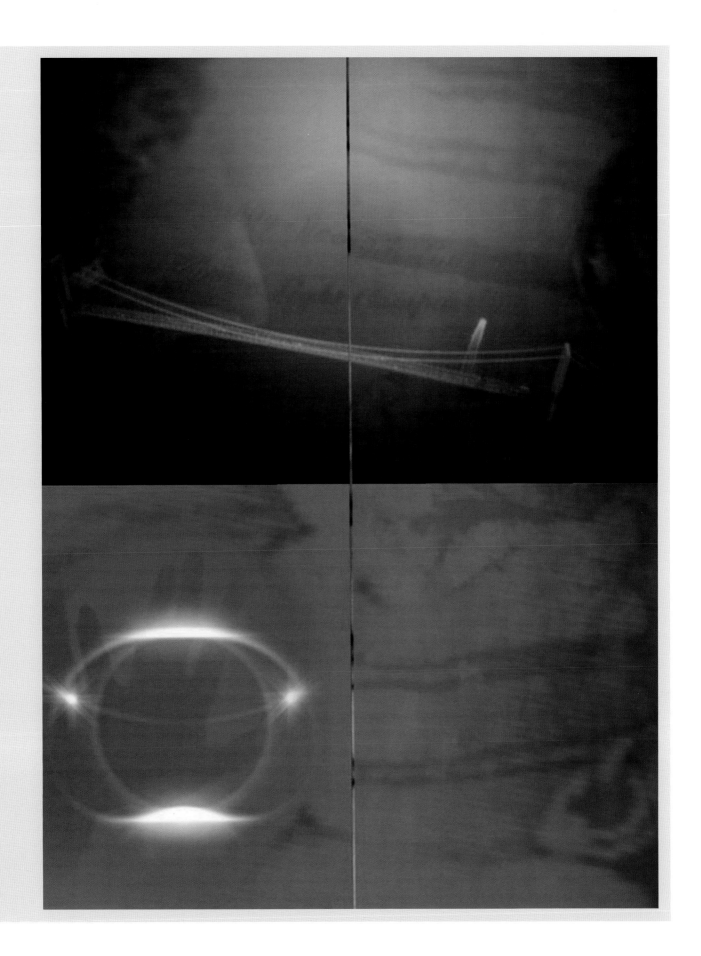

Eye and Hand

BY MIKE HIGHMEAD
Artist, Photographer
London, United Kingdom

For artist Mike Highmead, the
iPhone and iPad are a virtual
playground for his unconscious
mind to express itself.

Three pictures of a landscape, a hand and an eye
were processed using the infrared setting of the app
'CameraBag'.

MIKE HIGHMEAD
iPhone Surreal + Zen and the Art of iPhone Photography

When we are newborn babies, one of the first things we become aware of are our own hands. We don't connect them as belonging to us. The mysterious eyes of our parents float in and out of our vision. The Surrealists recognized how the eye could induce in us a memory of this state of primal wonder: a state we need to return to with more frequency.

I keep a library of images on my mobile devices to create with. Just playing around with the different art and photo apps can result in inspiration and some interesting imagery, and I'm often surprised at what emerges. Sometimes it feels as though I'm connecting directly with the unconscious, and in that respect it can be really therapeutic.

I also like the natural feeling of working with my fingers directly on the screen and the ease of uploading artwork straight to an online gallery and the world.

Using the app 'Juxtaposer', the landscape was opened as the background image, and the hand as the foreground image. The hand was cut out using the eraser tool, resized, rotated and positioned over the landscape.

Next, the eye image was opened as a new foreground picture and the same steps were followed.

Last, it was given a black frame using the app 'Photogene', to arrive at the final image.

it's closer than you think

BY MIKE HIGHMEAD
Artist, Photographer
London, United Kingdom

Mike Highmead is a photographer who has chosen these new tools to capture and express his own layers of reality, the subconscious mind and the Zen-like moments in time and space where the creative spirit soars, and he shares these experiences with us.

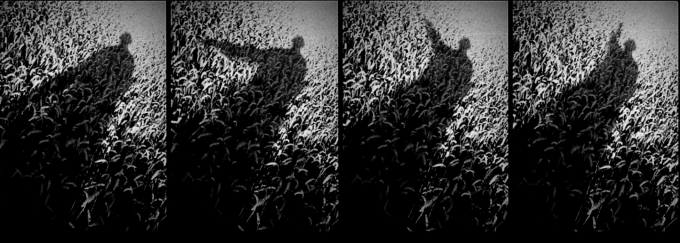

it's closer than you think, taken with the app 'QuadCamera', set on 4 x 1 layout and HI-CON setting.

Since practising Zen meditation, I've found that photography can become part of my practice. The act of looking and taking a picture in its purest form is profoundly simple, not unlike the Zen exercise of painting an enso circle, where a space is contained by a border.

By cultivating mindfulness in order to be 'in the moment', spontaneity and inspiration will sometimes come out of the blue.

It's possible for a feeling of unity to be achieved where photographer, camera and subject fuse together and a glimpse of a deeper reality is revealed.

The results can be self-illuminating, as in this shot, it's closer than you think, which on reflection reminded me of the Zen paradox of striving not to strive.

IPHONE DUCHAMP

iPhone Duchamp

BY DAVID SCOTT LEIBOWITZ
Artist, Technician, App Developer
New Jersey, USA

Like any new art form, mobile digital art is evolving technically, with the introduction of new apps every day, and philosophically, with artists from different perspectives and different cultures coming to the medium. In this tutorial, we will take a screenshot of the most famous painting on earth, and use four apps, "Kaleido", "iDoodle", "Collage", and "Polarize", to create an image that demonstrates new techniques and conveys a new philosophy.

STEP 1

Open the app "Art", an education application that has text information and images such as this, Leonardo da Vinci's *Mona Lisa* or *La Giaconda* (1507).

STEP 2

A screen grab on the iPhone or the iPad is accomplished by holding the sleep button and the home button simultaneously, until you hear a click and see a flash. After the flash, you can now find the image in your camera roll and open it in any photo/art app.

STEP 3

The screen grab was opened in the app "Kaleido", where you adjust the effect by swiping one or two fingers across the screen. I saved a number of variations to the camera roll and decided on using this variation as the background image.

STEP 4

The original screen grab is opened in the app "iDoodle2", where basic paint brushes are used to supply the graffiti, in the spirit of Dadaist Marcel Duchamp's famous *L.H.O.O.Q.* or *Joconde aux Moustaches* (1919). The image is then saved to the camera roll.

STEP 5

Open the app "Collage" and open the two previously saved elements. Position the foreground image on top of the background as shown, then save it to the camera roll.

The Dadaists, especially Duchamp with his famous L.H.O.O.Q. and his urinal, Fountain, infuriated the art establishment at the time, because they challenged the concept of "What is art?" Today, new challenges confront the art world as people from all walks of life pick up these mobile devices and make compelling art.

This is a "statement piece" for me, as it attempts to connect art history with this current explosion in art made on mobile devices.

STEP 6

The comp from Step 5 is opened in the app "Polarize", which adds the tint of an old Polaroid SX-70 and a classic white SX-70 frame.

Its caption feature looks as though it were hand-written with a Sharpie, which completes the piece in the true, irreverent spirit of Duchamp.

Ben on Stairs

BY DAVID SCOTT LEIBOWITZ
Artist, Technician, App Develo
New Jersey, USA

This example starts with good photograph taken a film set. It always helps any photo/art endeavor start with something goo This sounds simplistic, b I've found it to be true, th greatness in everythi requires a strong foundatio The steps involved to get final artwork are but a few, I've included many alternat final images. First, you'll s how a combination of ima and apps produces results th hit that dreamlike, surreal part of the brain in wa that cannot be predicte After that, we'll explore host of alternative creati opportunities.

STEP 1

Open the photo in the app "Face Melter" from the camera roll. Use one finger to push and twirl, or two fingers to pinch or expand: the photo is in a liquid state and can be moved around. You can modify the tool to return selected areas to their original state.

Original Photograph.

"Face Melter" Screenshot.

STEP 2

Save the altered image to the camera roll using the Share/Save to Device command.

These are three variations I created from the original photograph. The image on the previous page is my favorite for subliminal reasons, but it also has a clarity that makes it simple and compelling.

NOTE Film sets are designed and built by extremely talented people who made this photo possible. Set designers, carpenters, grips, props, and scenic artists all created this amazingly beautiful set piece, which was then lit by a director of photography, a gaffer, the electric department, and a few more grips. Then I showed up with my iPhone to take this photo.

STEP 3

The altered photo is opened in the app "ezimba", which provides hundreds of looks and presets. This is a combination of the presets Impressionist Sketch and Lightly Painted, and I also blended in "ezimba" to get the grainy, textured look that finalizes the piece.

When you break up photographic lines, the brain of the viewer ceases to perceive the image as a photograph, a lesson learned in the 1970s by pushing fluid SX-70 emulsion around. I added some major grain texture and some dreamlike color to depict this surreal environment.

TIP For those familiar with these kinds of digital liquefy tools from early versions of "Kai's Power Tools", "Painter", and then "Photoshop", this app will be very familiar. Go back further to the late 1970s, pre-digital, when the free-flowing Polaroid SX-70 emulsion allowed for a similar kind of image manipulation.

TIP To view legacy Polaroid SX-70 art: http://www.leibo.net/polaroid/.

Sometimes an exceptional image lends itself to multiple versions, as is the case with this one, where its journey takes a turn through different apps, variations to be realized as their own piece of distinctive art. This page will allow you to see how the power of one good image can assert itself through multiple apps.

There are over a half a million apps now. Rather than list my favorite apps, I took the photo from Step 2, which had been saved to my camera roll, and created variations showing what I love so much about creating art on mobile devices. Every day, the App Store has new offerings, most unrelated to your personal interest and then, "BOOM!!!", a new app appears that changes the way you approach your art, even for a day, even for an hour. Then it goes into your digital toolbox for the moment you really need it. Each app has controls and variations that allow for individual artistic interpretation, so the examples that follow are but a fraction of the infinite possibilities. Priceless!

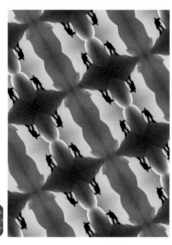

hallow this ground. The brave men
and dead, who struggled here have
consecrated it, far above
from the earth.

Original iPhone photograph, shot out the window of my car driving over the Midtown Bridge in Hackensack, NJ.

Milo's Bad Dream

BY DAVID SCOTT LEIBOWITZ
Artist, Technician, App Developer
New Jersey, USA

I created a surrealist collage using three original photographs, a screenshot from Safari and the apps "Collage" and "Juxtaposer". Half the lesson is: if you can think of it, you can do it, the tools are there, even if it's imagining you are exploring a cat's subconscious.

STEP 1

I begin by cropping the original in the app "Collage". I open the river view image and, using two fingers, expand the image to fill the vertical frame as shown. I make sure to think about the horizon line. It's right now I need to visualize the final framing, so I can leave room for the foreground elements.

This is the base image on which we will build our final collage.

STEP 2

Still in "Collage", add sleeping Milo image to the base image and change its level of transparency to 60 percent. I size it so the top edge of the Milo frame lines up perfectly with the shoreline for a perfect transition. Save the file to the camera roll.

Original photo, Milo Milowitz dreaming kitty dreams.

STEP 3

Open the second photo in the app "Face Melter". Pinch with two fingers, or push with one to move Milo's features and create this version below, "Evil Milo". Save the file to your camera roll.

Second iPhoto of Milo, charming home-wrecker, destroyer of antiquities.

STEP 4

Open the app "Juxtaposer", and open the background image from Step 2. When prompted, open "Evil Milo" as the top image. Using the eraser, subtract everything from the image but the cat. By zooming in using a two-fingered motion. you can cut a very precise shape, in this case one evil-looking cat.

TIP This process of cutting a precise shape is best accomplished by using a stylus, like a Ten/One pogo or Nomad brush. This will allow you to easily see exactly where you're erasing.

STEP 5

Still in the app "Juxtaposer" and using the same two-fingered motion, I resize the cat and then save the cat as a stamp. First I position the top cat layer to the right and, using the "Stamp Top Image" command, repeat the evil cat element and position it slightly to the left. Repeat this step two more times, then save this version to your camera roll.

STEP 6

I open Safari, search "Gettysburg Address", and find one in Abe Lincoln's handwriting. Capture a screenshot, using the home button and sleep button on the iPhone or iPad. The screenshot is saved to your camera roll.

STEP 7

I open the previous screenshot in the app "Collage" and zoom in with my fingers so it fills the frame. (This Lincoln's Gettysburg Address is what appeared to Milo in his nightmare.) Then I add the saved version from Step 5, slightly skewed to throw the composition off balance. Remember, I am going for surrealism here, so I don't want the viewer to get too comfortable.

STEP 8

I change the level of transparency of the top image to 50 percent. I'm looking to depict a cat's nightmare, so ambiguity rules.

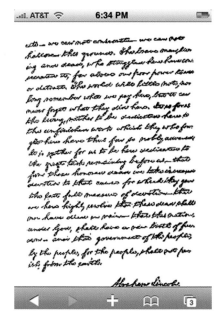

STEP 9

I add the same final saved image from Step 5, smaller, skewed even more this time and now at 100 percent transparency, to complete the final collage. Sometimes, adding more than one off-balance element creates a newfangled balance to the final composition.

I have taken a photo of the Hackensack river, two photos of our cat Milo, and a screenshot of the Gettysburg Address to create this surrealist collage. The Dadaists, just before the Surrealists, loved using appropriated objects and images in their art. They would have appreciated the iPhone and iPad's ability to appropriate anything you could think of and use it to make art.

Magic hour in Times Square (opposite) is perfect for the app "Pro HDR". HDR stands for high dynamic range, capturing details in the highlight areas of the photo first, then a second exposure to capture the details in the shadows. The app combines the two exposures, as shown above, creating a photo that is closer to the way we actually see the world around us.

I opened the image below in the app "PhotoViva" where I painted it using abstract and cloning brushes to add and subtract brush strokes and original details. The functionality of this app allows me to rework my photographs the exact same way I've done it for almost twenty years in the desktop application "Painter".

Tourist with Statue of Liberty, painted in "PhotoViva".

Apps (Times) Squared

BY DAVID SCOTT LEIBOWITZ
Artist, Technician, App Developer
New Jersey, USA

Creating art in Times Square is like shooting fish in a barrel. At first, it overwhelms your senses and then it's like butter.

After three years of writing this book, the day before my final deadline I decided to have some fun and create a chapter in my favorite place on earth. Enjoy!

The app "Photosynth" allows you to create seamless, 360 degree images. Within "Photosynth"'s viewer and their website, this 2D image can be navigated immersively, like "Quick-Time VR".

The app "Photastic HD" has a vast array of selective particle controls.

The app "Tiny Planets" creates stereographic projections from your photos (right). Twenty years ago, you would have needed a supercomputer to accomplish this effect.

The app "3D Photo" allows you to map your photos onto various 3D shapes or grids.

The app "Luminancer" has multiple modes and settings to control the amount of image lag in your photos.

The photo was painted onto this 3D cube in the app "123D Sculpt".

The app "3D PhotoCut" allowed me to isolate this colorful NYC character from a very busy background.

 Named "You Gotta See This!", this app creates Hockney-esque collages by pointing your mobile device up and down and all around to capture the scene.

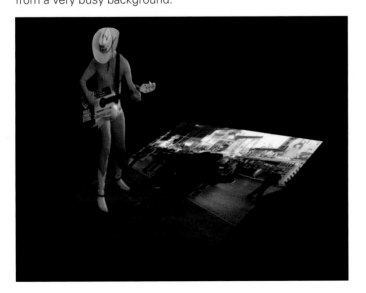

Times Square offers up the visual energy and then it's up to you. Armed with my iPhone, a few of my favorite apps and I'm good to go!

Section 3

Abstract, Background, and Conceptual Apps

There are many apps that generate abstract art. This section will look at some of the most useful ones that should be in everyone's toolbox and a few others just to get you thinking.

It should be noted, here, that there are dedicated artists who choose to spend their entire supply of creative energy exploring these apps to the nth degree. This is their artform, the search for beauty in abstract visualizations and, perhaps, the subject of another book.

My goal here is to round out this very large group of apps to the most relevant and the ones mobile artists have gravitated to as part of their digital toolbox. The goal is to also provide an insightful visual overview so the prospective artist can effectively determine their possible value to his/her own iPhone/iPad art.

They include apps that are interactive fractal generators, kaleidoscope apps that allow for transformations of any image on your camera roll, abstract image-generating apps of various types, 3D modeling apps, and apps that let you paint like Jackson Pollock or Mark Rothko. The section also includes apps that are designed to transform your photos in various abstract ways.

This section concludes with examples of apps that were created as art pieces, so that the art is the experience of interacting with the app, not necessarily the outcome. Created by artists who have taken up this new challenge, they force us to wrap our heads around the very concept of app as art. The section ends with a chapter where the iPhone itself is the artwork and with some final thought-provoking ideas on "What is art?" as it relates to mobile devices.

Fractals

I use the apps "iFractals" and "Fractal 3D" to create Mandlebrot or Julia set abstract images. These are essentially visual representations of complex mathematical equations. They are compelling images into themselves, but I use them for backgrounds, or elements in a collage.

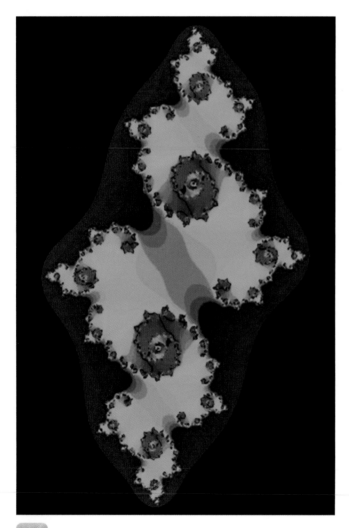

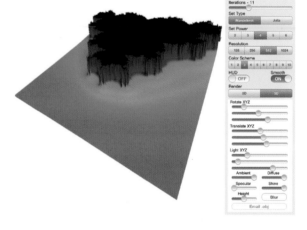

"Fractal 3D" has enough settings to satisfy the biggest app brainiac and creates amazingly beautiful images based on mathematics.

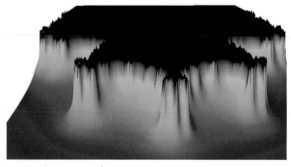

Kaleidoscopes

To create kaleidoscopic variations of photographs or any image you can pull from your camera roll, I use the apps "Kooleido" and "Kaleido".

NOTE   Some variations are saved to the camera roll to be used in future collages while some stand alone as final artwork, to be uploaded, printed, exhibited, and sold.

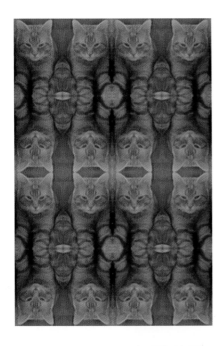

Abstract Art Generators

The app "Artisan" is an abstract image generator whose visual parameters are determined by your gestures with one, two, or three fingers. At times, it is like playing a musical instrument. A number of mobile artists, particularly Helene Goldberg and Patricio Villarroel, have integrated elements created in "Artisan" into their iPhone and iPad art. Examples of images created in "Artisan" are shown opposite and below.

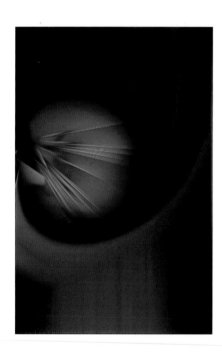

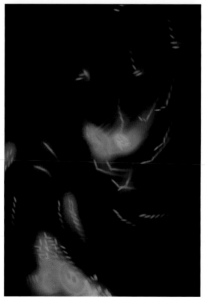

"Spawn Glow" is an app that creates a swarm of colored lights that follow the touch of your finger, creating a light show and images that are compelling and beautiful.

"iBeams HD" interactive visualizer reacts to your touch or pinch plus the beat and volume of your music.

"Meshmerizer" generates abstract planes of color by touch or by sound.

The app "magic donut" has settings to create various undulating 3D shapes.

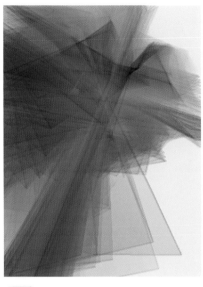

"SculptMaster 3D" is a very basic 3D app that lets you paint and carve a clay-like material in a 3D space to create unique 3D objects, but throws in an unlimited amount of fun. The artist Kara Jansson Kovacev uses this app in her chapter to create basic head shapes which she then paints in "Brushes".

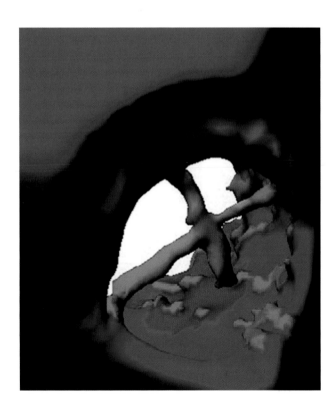

 The app "Meritum Paint" paints with a furry brush or with neon particles that follow your finger's path, and creates paintings with an organic, abstract feeling.

 The app "Artree" has masses of controls that allow you to grow trees of different types, with foliage and flower controls.

"Iamascope HD" is an app that allows you to import images as parts of a moving kaleidoscope. It creates 3D objects that move around the frame controlled by your finger movements.

Not to be outdone, the app "Roth-komatic" lets you create complex Rothko-like compositions like the one shown above.

The app "Jackson Pollock" lets you paint on a blank canvas or any image from your camera roll with drippy, Pollock-like brush strokes.

The app "Deco Sketch" provides a unique set of brushes and its own look.

Photo Abstractions

"Fracture" has graphic cloning brushes that help you create Cubist renditions from your photos.

"Abstract Me" creates a mask that combines with your photos and a library of textures in unusual ways to create some very unique looks.

Open a photo in the app "Photo Mosaica", define image folders to draw photos from, and the app creates an amazingly high resolution mosaic.

"Photastic HD" is a powerful image manipulation tool with Liquefy and Shatter modes shown above. There are effect and restore brushes to control the placement and exact amount of manipulation.

"123D Sculpt" has 3D models you can alter, paint with your photos, then animate and reposition in 3D space.

"WordFoto" allows you to create a collage made of text you enter into the app with your photo (see above).

"Decim8", above, has infinite variations of visual glitches that you can apply to your photos. This app doubles as a fine art app, which leads us to the next group.

David Scott Leibowitz **311**

The App as Art …

To use the app "Satromizer", simply touch the screen where a glitch is desired. Multiple fingers can be used to glitch more than one area at a time. Image files are typically read from top to bottom; the area of the picture that is touched coincides with the data to be scrambled.

"Satromizer" image by Ben Syverson.

Jon Satrom: "Glitches are unexpected events that momentarily expose the systems at play. I appreciate when things go wrong. It makes one step back for a moment and consider context."

Fire before and after "Satromizer".

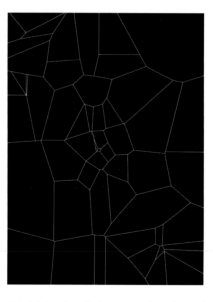

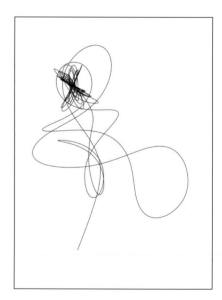

"Bubble Harp" by app developer/ techno artist Scott Snibbe combines music and a harp-like visualization to create a Zen-like, interactive art app experience.

Another Scott Snibbe app called "Tripolar" is a simple yet compellingly beautiful piece of interactive app art.

Another Lia app "PhiLia 01" is about artistic harmony, expressed through interactive movements and touch. You set various parameters, then touch and tilt the iPad or iPhone to create movement within the image. The software and the user collaborate to define the creative experience from session to session.

"Arcs 21" was originally an online software art project by Austrian artist Lia, where the interaction with the elements alters the image in an infinite number of ways.

"For All Seasons" by Andreas Müller is a combination of poetry and visual art that is affected by touch. The viewer interacts with the letters that compose the poem and views the interaction from any 3D viewpoint he/she chooses.

The Small Glass (after Duchamp), 2009

BY ETHAN HAM
Conceptual Artist, Professor
Egremont, Massachusetts

Conceptual art and art history merge in the accident that is broken glass.

Born and raised in Iowa, I studied at the University of California at Santa Cruz and Portland State University (Portland, Oregon). I now live in Massachusetts and I'm an artist and an associate professor of new media at the City College of New York.

I often explore themes of translation and mutation. My projects include literary / art hybrids, kinetic sculptures, and internet-based artworks.

My artistic influences are Marcel Duchamp, Jean Tinguely, and Tim Hawkinson. The iPhone artwork I created directly references / appropriates Duchamp's The Bride Stripped Bare by Her Bachelors, Even *(also known as* The Large Glass*).*

On my wedding day, I plugged my iPhone into the restaurant's sound system to play music during the reception dinner. My bride and I were leaving the venue when I realized the phone was still playing music. I juggled the phone out of my pocket, dropped it on the cobblestone sidewalk, and cracked the glass.

Perhaps the joy of the evening affected my outlook, but I immediately decided I liked—even preferred—the (literally) cracked iPhone. The phone still functions perfectly, but now it is unique. Besides the formal aesthetic of the cracked glass, I find a moralistic gratification in continuing to use the phone—the crack counters the sense of conspicuous consumption I used to feel every time I pulled out the phone.

The pleasure I found in the cracked glass reminded me of Marcel Duchamp's *The Bride Stripped Bare by Her Bachelors, Even*—a work that is also known as *The Large Glass*. This glass artwork accidently cracked while being transported. When repairing it, Duchamp decided that he liked the chance element of the cracks and kept them as part of the work.

ETHAN HAM

The Small Glass (after Duchamp)

Very shortly after cracking the iPhone, I downloaded a photograph of *The Large Glass* and set it as my wallpaper. Whenever a bystander comments on my iPhone's cracked glass (which happens fairly frequently), I say that it is an artwork. Sometimes I go as far as explaining that it is a "readymade aided". *The Small Glass (after Duch-amp)* is an artwork that is not on, but of, an iPhone.

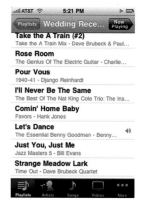

Prior to my wedding, I had been planning to make some iPhone-based artwork and had been playing around with programming the phone. Before becoming an artist, I worked in the computer game industry as a game designer and programmer, so an interactive iPhone artwork seemed a natural path. But in the end, a Duch-ampian gesture of declaring the phone itself an artwork satisfied my desire to create something that uses the unique characteristics of the phone.

There are many reasons to create artwork on an iPhone. It's a pocket-sized art studio, it can be done in a dark environment, it's challenging, it's new, and it's fun to fingerpaint.

Any one of these reasons can be the answer to "Why do it on an iPhone?" But it's worth repeating the question and thinking about creating artworks that resonate with the phone around them.

The other day I was riding on the subway and noticed a passenger who was passing the time by drawing on his iPhone. One great aspect of the iPhone is being able to cleanly undo any unwanted marks. This allowed the subway artist to erase the evidence of the subway car's bounce and jiggle from his drawing. But he could have equally embraced the chance motion and made it part of the artwork—an acknowledgement that a key characteristic of the iPhone is its portability. Such a drawing would bring to mind William Anastasi's Subway Drawings, in which his hand acted as a seismograph that translated the subway's movement onto a sheet of paper.

Taking artistic advantage of a technological advance does not need to result in gimmickry. The 19th century saw the development of manufactured tubes of paint. Tubes of paint may seem an innocuous innovation, but in accepting the convenience of no longer needing to grind their own pigments, artists relinquished their absolute control of color. Being limited to a mixture of industry-specified colors is restricting in the same way that digital artists are constrained by the pixel and the RGB slider. As Duchamp said, "Since the tubes of paint used by the artists are manufactured and readymade products we must conclude that all paintings in the world are 'readymades aided' and also works of assemblage."

Undoubtedly there were artists who railed against the use of manufactured paint, but the tubes (along with the invention of the portable box easel) gave artists a freedom of movement that encouraged them to step out of their studios and into plein air. There is little point in painting outside if it does not have some impact on the resulting art, so artists began trying to capture the moment and its light in paintings that were dashed off in one quick session. Impressionism was born. Perhaps some characteristic or consequence of the iPhone will lead somewhere as unexpected and interesting.

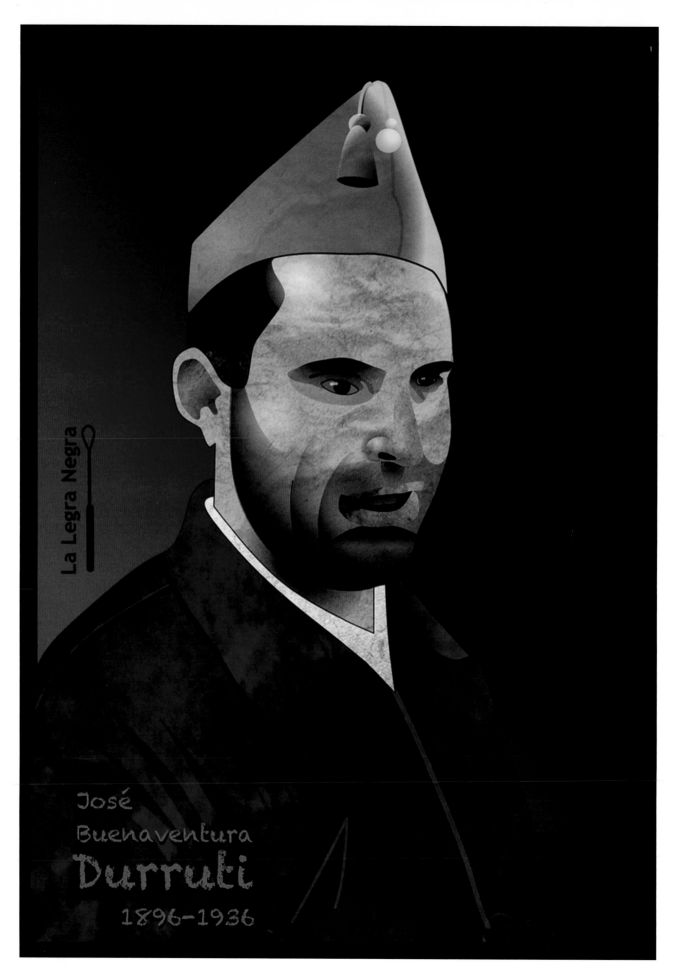

La Legra Negra

José
Buenaventura
Durruti
1896-1936

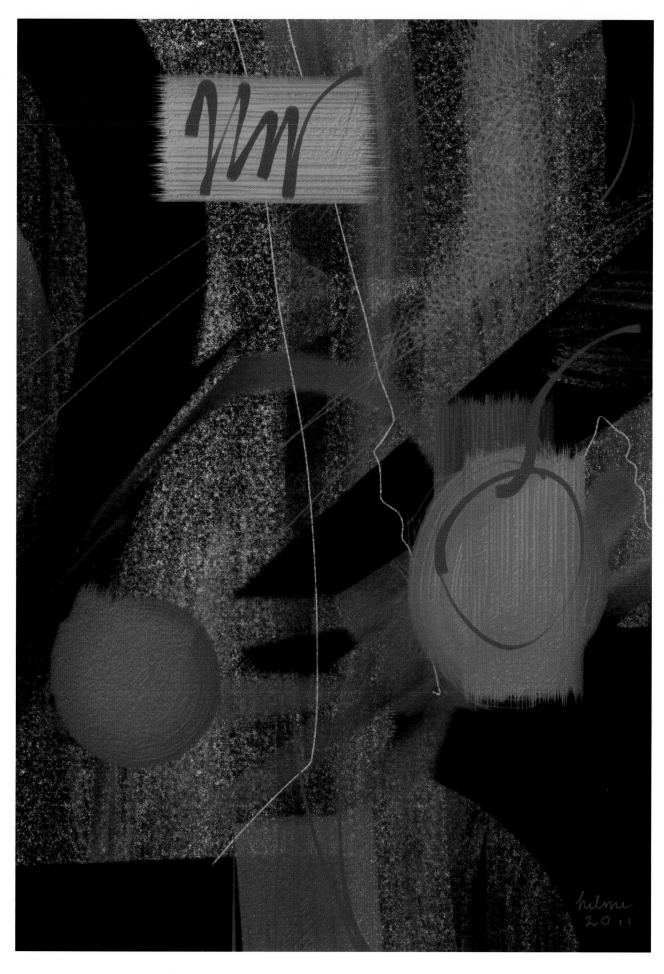

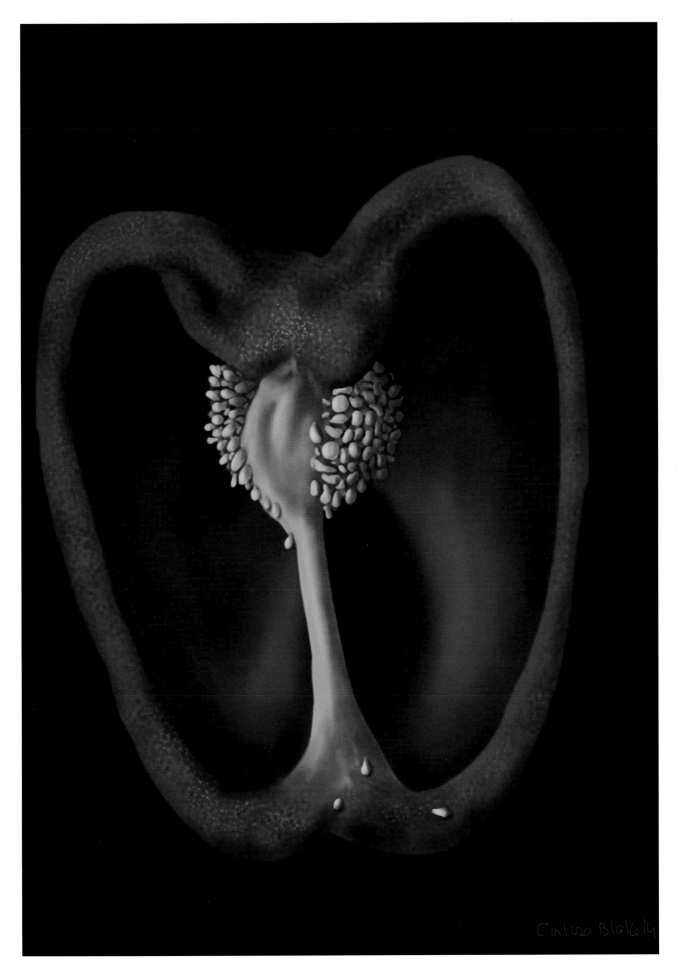

ARTISTS' GALLERY: Corliss Blakely **335**

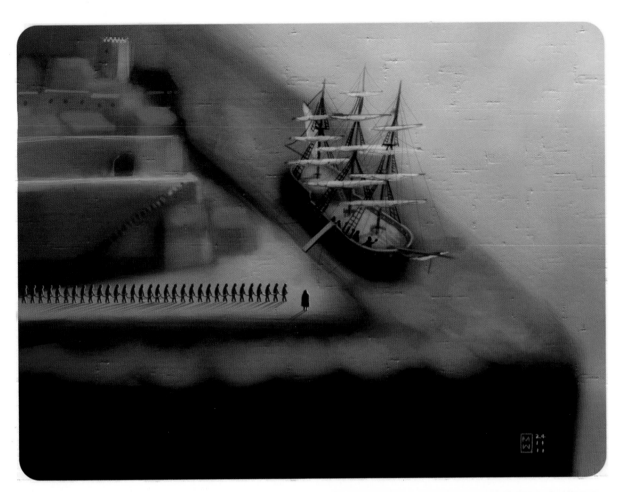

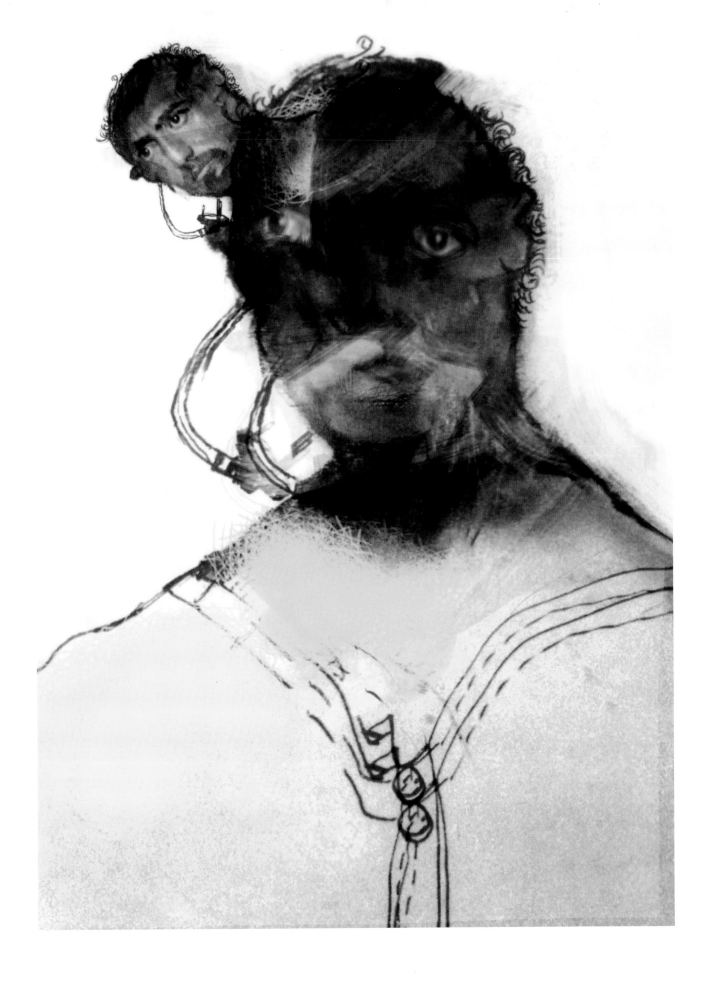

CONTRIBUTING ARTISTS

Alex · Amy · Andrea · Barbara · Ben · Benjamin · Benoit · Betsy · Borja

Cédric · Christine · Cindy · Corliss · Craig · Dan · David N · David S L · David

Deborah · Ethan · Gabriel · Helene · Iquanyin · Jan · Joey · John · Jose A G P

Jose C · Julian · Kara · Kevin · Knox · Kyle · Lucy · Luis · Maia

Marcella · Mathieu · Matthew S C · Matthew W · Mic · Michael I · Michael G · Miguel · Mike H

Mike M · Mike N · Necojita · Nini · Patricio · Rita · Robert · Roberta · Russ

Salvador · Sam · Sean · Stéphane · Thierry · Thomas · Tony · Valerie · William

Willie · Xoan